I0099354

THE
DARK HORSE
MINDSET

Take Control, Own Your Value, and Win in Life

GERALD ESMAILZADEH

GERALD ESMAILZADEH

© Copyright 2025. Gerald Esmailzadeh. All rights reserved.

No part of this publication may be reproduced, stored in a retrieval system, or transmitted in any form or by any means, electronic, mechanical, photocopying, recording, or otherwise, without the prior written permission of the author, except in the case of brief quotations used for review, educational purposes, or non-commercial use permitted by copyright law.

This book is a work of original content created by Gerald Esmailzadeh. All content, including but not limited to text, design, layout, graphics, and original ideas, are the intellectual property of the author and are protected under international copyright law.

Unauthorized reproduction or distribution of this material is prohibited and may result in legal action.

This publication is intended for personal use and educational purposes only. It is not intended to serve as professional advice, therapy, counseling, or any form of professional guidance. The author disclaims any liability from the use or misuse of the information contained within.

AUTHOR: GERALD ESMAILZADEH

ISBN-13: 979-8889370659

"Life is unfair until I make life fair for me"

- Gerald Esmailzadeh

TABLE OF CONTENTS

INTRODUCTION

"The old you doesn't define the future you." — **Anonymous**

Ever questioned if you're on the right path? Felt like you're just existing instead of truly living?

I think we've all felt that at some point in our lives.

It was nearing midnight. I stood on a busy street in the heart of the city, right in front of a high-end hotel. At this hour, I was exhausted, but I kept knocking on car windows and handing out flyers.

I remember wearing a white polo barong that I'd bought at a local store, a pair of black pants, and leather shoes that seemed to be wearing out.

The heat was brutal, sweat pouring down my face. All I had for company was the endless hustle and bustle of the city. That was my life, day in and day out.

"Was I just not good enough?"

"Is this really my destiny?

These thoughts kept bouncing around in my head as I knocked on each car that rolled by, tapping at their windows.

This had been my life for the last 6 months.

And nothing was happening...

I was telling my girlfriend (who is now my wife) how terrified I was of losing this job. In real estate, you've got 6 months, max, to prove your worth.

"Am I not worthy of a sale?"

Just to get through, I constantly reminded myself that every person who accepts my flyer is a potential 60,000 pesos in my pocket.

Was there any chance of a breakthrough, or was this just the beginning of the end?

The next day, my manager sent me to a massive, well-known mall across the city. I arrived there at around 10 am, and I stayed there until closing.

Nothing special about that day. Just handed out flyers, doing my usual rounds.

At around 8:45 pm, I was getting ready to go home. The day was almost done, and I still had the same feeling as the day before, defeated. I thought to myself, maybe it's time I give this up and time to choose another job, or probably even go back to modeling, but at my age, that wouldn't be the most practical solution.

At that moment, there was a certain level of acceptance in my heart that maybe this path was not for me.

So, I started packing up, clearing our booth, until I saw a lady from afar, about 200 meters away.

I couldn't explain it, but something about her drew me in, urging me to approach her.

The place was clearing out, people were leaving, so what did I have to lose?

When you have nothing to lose anymore, you have so much to gain in the end.

"Hi mam, my name is Gerald Esmailzadeh. We have a real estate project here in the city, in case you would be interested."

"Oh really? So, it's a prime spot?"

"Yes, mam."

"When can you show me this project?"

"Well mam, if you like, I can show this to you tonight if you're available."

"That's perfect. I'm leaving for the US tomorrow night. Can you bring me to the showroom?"

I was shocked at her immediate response. It was something I didn't expect. We drove from the mall to the showroom, about 15–20-minute travel time.

Looking back, I had no idea that this seemingly insignificant encounter would become one of the most pivotal experiences of my life. After that night, this lady and I developed a friendship. I later found out that she'd graduated Magna Cum Laude at the age of 17, with two majors in Accounting and Management, from a reputable university. She even passed the CPA exam at the age of 18 and earned her master's with a degree in Marketing and Management.

A Certified Public Accountant and a multimillionaire in dollars.

By the time we got to the showroom, it was already closed, so I asked the guard if he could open it for us.

I saw his hesitation, but he said, "Sir, the showroom is closed, but I will open it for you, just for tonight."

Maybe it was some kind of cosmic intervention, who knows? I'm not sure what made him do it, but I was damn grateful.

We opened the showroom and after I presented her with the project, she got up and was ready to leave. Then, she faced me and said, "I'll go back tomorrow morning, and I'll let you know my decision then."

The next day, she met me at our office in Makati just before her flight and, to my surprise, decided to buy two units on the spot.

After 6 long months of despair and countless rejections, I had finally made a sale!

A few days later, she called again. This time, she wanted to purchase an entire floor of the project.

And the rest, as they say, is history...

At this point, you're probably wondering who I am, and what makes me so special to write a book.

Well, just like you, I am trying to survive in this thing called Life. I am not special nor was I gifted with special powers.

But the one thing I can share with you, and something I'm proud of and perhaps the whole purpose of this book, is my story and how you can turn any adversity into an opportunity.

It's about adopting what I call the "Dark Horse Mindset", that relentless drive to prove doubters wrong and achieve success against all odds.

Just like a dark horse in a race, often dismissed at the start, I've learned to harness my inner strength and defy expectations.

As a salesman, my journey wasn't about selling products; it started with selling myself, my skills, my passion, and my vision.

And that's where true success begins.

I wrote this book because, honestly, I wish someone had written it for me when I was struggling. I didn't have a roadmap, a guide, or a mentor when I faced my own struggles. I know firsthand how isolating and overwhelming it can feel to get through life's challenges without a clear path forward.

That's why I wrote this book, to offer you that shortcut I didn't have, the guidance, the helping hand I so desperately needed back then.

I believe that everyone encounters difficulties in life, and sometimes all we need is a little push, a reminder that we're not alone, and a glimpse of what's possible.

This book is about my journey and the lessons I've learned. I hope it inspires you to find that inner strength, that "dark horse" spirit we all have inside us and use it to create the life you truly want.

If my story can provide that for even one person, then this book will have served its purpose.

This story right here, marked my breakthrough. As I was on the verge of giving up, hope arrived in the most unexpected way.

This right here, amplified my dreams. I realized that if you put in the work and believe in yourself, then nothing is impossible.

Life is a series of choices. Sometimes, we get it wrong, but there's always a chance to course-correct. There's always tomorrow to try again. The power to choose is yours.

The question is: Will you choose to keep reading, to explore the possibilities within these pages, or will you let this moment pass you by, and stay where you are?

Like I said, the choice is yours.

PART ONE

BUILDING YOUR CONFIDENCE:
BUILDING THE BETTER
VERSION OF **YOU**

CHAPTER ONE

Self-Awareness

"How much can you know about yourself if you've never been in a fight?" — **Tyler Durden, Fight Club**

I was 21 when my mom died.

It was May 1, 2005. The city was alive with fiesta celebrations, but my world was falling apart.

I was on the phone with my girlfriend, sitting beside my mom. She had been bedridden for two months as cancer had finally taken over. After a few minutes, I decided to move to the sofa across the room. I glanced at my mom and saw that her chest was no longer moving.

"Mom's not breathing."

I hung up, my hand shaking. I knew it was coming, but it still hit like a punch to the gut. Nothing prepares you for the moment death happens.

I went to her, held her in my arms, and kissed her goodbye. I immediately called all my relatives. The ambulance came, and I saw them carry her away. They were taking her to the hospital, but I knew that was just a protocol.

At first, I felt fine. Her death hadn't sunk in yet. But after the burial, everything crashed. My world just... stopped.

My mind went blank. My confidence, my sense of security, was gone. My mom was my biggest believer, and without her, I felt like I had lost a part of myself. I never met my dad, and now the only person who ever truly had my back was gone.

This wasn't the first time I had to fend for myself. I started modeling at 18, working with different brands. Back when my mom was around, I had the luxury of choosing my projects. And I'd only take gigs with big names that paid well and helped me build my reputation and network in the industry.

But when she passed away, I had no other choice but to survive.

I took any gig I could get my hands on. If it kept me in the game, put some cash in my pocket, and helped my modeling career, I was all in.

However, I soon came to realize how unstable the income was in this industry. I booked big projects sometimes, but the competition was fierce. Brazilian models were taking over, with better looks, better bodies, and much cheaper rates than us. I loved modeling. The glamour, the excitement, it was all a rush. But let's be real, it wasn't exactly a solid career plan.

Then my girlfriend hit me with the truth: "You can't be a model forever."

I wanted to be in this industry, even dreaming of becoming an actor someday. When I first started out, things were looking good. I'd been doing commercials and print ads for major brands. I also got the opportunity to land a cameo role in a series. But the game had changed. It was getting harder and harder to book gigs.

That's when I started to realize that maybe my dreams were out of reach. It was a tough pill to swallow, but it forced me to take a hard look at myself and my skills. I had to figure out what else I was good at, and what other paths I could take.

Then one day, one of my model friends asked me if I would like to try real estate.

I'm not the type of person to quit, to give up, but I had to face reality.

I didn't give up on my modeling dreams; I just put it on hold because I needed something steady to pay the bills. So, I gave real estate a shot. I'd still do the occasional VTR, but it just wasn't the same. It felt like the magic was gone, like I wasn't getting the breaks I used to.

When I was starting out in real estate, money was a bit tight without my mom. My girlfriend had just started her new job. I even remember that every morning we would buy a McDonald's breakfast sandwich together, and split it in two, just to get by.

Still, I thought that this was life's way of pushing me in a new direction. Sometimes, things don't go according to plan, and that's okay. It might even be a blessing in disguise. What seems like a detour could be the real path after all.

I figured, for now, I needed to focus on something that could put food on the table. But I also wanted it to feel right, to make it meaningful. And in real estate, I realized it was still kind of like modeling. You're not just selling houses or condos, but you're selling yourself. It's about building relationships and showing people; you genuinely care about helping them find their dream home. You must be confident, know your stuff, and be persuasive, and it's just like on the runway or in a commercial. It's about letting your personality shine through, showing your passion, and proving that you're committed to getting the job done.

This is what, I guess you can say, pushed me to be more aware of my strengths, and my weaknesses. This redirection helped me discover things that I am good at, and things I needed to improve.

Come to think of it, my desire of wanting to improve wasn't internal; it stemmed from having nothing and wanting to have the finer things in life. My drive came from those who doubted me, from those naysayers, those who judged me and told me that I wouldn't make it. Yes, they were my motivation, and as bad as it sounds, it worked for me.

If people doubt you, it's on you to prove them wrong. That's the dark horse mentality right there. Coming from where I did, with nothing to my name, I was fueled by that underdog spirit. I was damn sure I was gonna show everyone what I was made of.

I think a lot of that drive came from my childhood. Growing up, it was just me and my mom. We didn't have much, just the basics. But my mom's side of the family? They were living the high life. My uncles, aunts, cousins... they had money. My mom didn't have that luxury. As the eldest daughter, she had to take care of her parents. She worked a regular job while they had successful businesses. My cousins went to fancy schools here and overseas and wore designer clothes like Versace and Gucci. Meanwhile, my mom and I were just scraping by.

And yeah, I'll admit it, I was envious, but not at them, but at the situation. I didn't like how my mom and I had less compared to our relatives. I'm not usually the envious type, but that was the one time in my life I felt it.

I remember that every time we would go to a family reunion in a posh neighborhood where my relatives lived, all of them would roll up in their cars, all shiny and new. My mom and I?

We'd be squeezing onto a packed bus or jeepney, and lucky if we could afford a cab.

I'll never forget those times when it was pouring with rain, and I'd watch my mom fighting her way onto a jeepney, getting jostled around. It was heartbreaking. I told her, "One day, we won't have to do this anymore. We'll have our own car, and we won't have to struggle like this."

But my mom, she never let that get to her. She'd always say, "At the end of the day, if you work hard, the Lord will always reward you." That's something I'll never forget. She taught me the value of hard work, that if you want something, you got to hustle for it.

And she lived by that, too. If she wanted to buy something, she'd save every penny, even skip meals if she had to. I remember once that she wanted to buy a television, and she saved up like crazy just so she could afford it. When I wanted a new pair of shoes, she told me to save up my allowance so I could buy them for myself. It was tough love, but it taught me a valuable lesson, and this mindset was something that shaped me as a person.

There was a time when I lived by myself, not by choice, but by circumstance. You see, I was only 10 years old when my mom brought me to a cool, misty mountain town because the doctor said the fresh air would help my asthma. But since she still had to work in the busy, traffic-choked capital, I had no choice but to stay behind. She would visit once a week to check up on me, then head back to the city shortly after.

Everything was so foreign to me. My mom placed me in an apartment, but we didn't know anyone there. There was no referral. We had no relation with the landlord or with any of the tenants.

My mom had asked a store in front of the apartment to keep a credit for my expenses monthly, and she would pay for it. When she would visit, she would give me my weekly allowance so that I could do my own grocery shopping.

With all the extra expenses, and being a single mom, she had to hustle even harder. So, whenever she'd visit me, she'd bring Suka (vinegar) or patis (fish sauce) from the city to sell there. Then, on her way back, she'd stock up on those everlasting flowers to sell back home.

I saw it all firsthand. I witnessed both worlds. The two worlds of these people having everything, and us having nothing. In fact, these were the things that made me the person I am today. These experiences built my mindset and my principles. It's what pushed me to work harder and smarter. I believe that knowing yourself and becoming self-aware is a huge factor to success. It's like having a compass, guiding you through life's twists and turns, helping you make choices that align with who you are and what you want to achieve.

When you truly know who you are, and know what you're capable of, life will go your way.

Take for instance a time when I was bullied. I remember that I was made fun of for my looks and the way I spoke. I looked different and even spoke differently, and locals could instantly tell I was from the city.

However, these kids loved playing Sipa, the Filipino game with a woven ball. I figured that if I wanted to fit in, if I wanted to get accepted, I had to get good at it. So, I practiced every day. And eventually, I got damn good. They started to see me differently. Plus, I'd sometimes treat them at the store (thanks to Mom's credit), and before I knew it, I was part of the gang.

Looking back, I see how all of that had a purpose. Imagine that at 10 years old, I was forced to live alone and survive, with no family or relatives. I realized the universe was preparing me for what was to come. If I was able to make it then, what makes me think that I won't be able to make it now that my mom is gone? Sure, things were different now, more responsibilities, but that same grit, that same determination, it was still there.

So, that was my life for a while. Until one day, everything changed. My mom got diagnosed with cancer, and I had to move back in with her.

All those experiences, from growing up with less to living alone, losing my mom, and hustling at a young age, forced me to look inward. That's where self-awareness comes in. It's about knowing yourself, your strengths and your weaknesses. You have to be honest with yourself, even if it's uncomfortable.

Self-awareness isn't just about comparing how you see yourself to how others see you. It's digging deeper, getting to know the real you: the good, the bad, and everything in between. It's about understanding what makes you tick, what gets you fired up, and where you might need to work on yourself a bit.

But to do that, you must be willing to look in the mirror and also be open to what others have to say about you. It's not always easy to hear, but sometimes the people around you can see things you can't.

When you put it all together, what you know about yourself and what others see, that's when you start to get the full picture. And that's when you can start making real changes, growing into the best version of yourself.

I remember the time when I started wakeboarding and hired a wakeboarder coach to train me. In wakeboarding, especially when you are a beginner, it is best to film yourself so that you can monitor your progress. One day, I excitedly showed my video to my coach. However, instead of giving feedback on my progress as a wakeboarder, he insulted the video that I edited. I was offended but at the same time challenged. In my mind, I told myself that I would prove him wrong. From then on, I constantly filmed and edited my wakeboarding sessions.

Then an idea hit me, why not make a wakeboarding video that's never been done before in the country?

I asked two of my wakeboarder friends to film me, and I'd handle the editing. Turns out, that video became the biggest Filipino wakeboarding video at the time. International magazines and websites picked it up because it was something fresh, from the editing to the music to the whole vibe.

Those insults, those failures... they were fuel for my ambition.

And then one day, a wakeboarder asked if I wanted to film a debut (coming-of-age party) and edit the video on the same day. I didn't know the first thing about filming a debut, but I took the gig. It was a gut feeling. From there, I did a wedding video, then another, and soon brands were reaching out to me. My portfolio was growing, and so was my confidence. Then later, I put up my own creative agency.

So, you see, if you're too scared to try new things, to get out of your comfort zone, then you'll never grow.

Adversity is like a mirror that forces you to see what you're truly made of. It's where you discover your limits and learn how to push past them.

Growth without a clear goal is just an aimless struggle. That's why having a goal, a purpose, is crucial. Without it, what are you even working toward? You must ask yourself, "What's my why?" What's the deeper reason behind what you're doing? If there's no real connection, no fire driving you forward, then what's the point?

And that's where the Dark Horse Mindset comes in. It's about resilience, about showing up even when everything in you wants to quit. It's about turning every failure, every rejection, every insult into fuel. Instead of letting doubt consume you, you use it as motivation to prove to yourself that you're capable of more.

People will doubt you. They'll tell you you're not good enough, not smart enough, not talented enough. Tune them out. Listen to your own inner voice. That's where your true path lies.

So, ask yourself: What does it take for you to truly know your strengths and weaknesses? Because self-awareness, knowing your real self, is the first step to becoming unstoppable.

You're not just here to exist. You're here to become something more. And that journey, the one that sets you apart from the rest? That's what it means to be the dark horse.

It's a never-ending journey, but trust me, it's worth it.

KEY TAKEAWAYS

- **Self-Awareness Is Your Foundation for Growth:** Knowing yourself inside and out is the first step to mastering life. But you can't do it alone. Your blind spots, those weaknesses or habits you don't notice, can only be revealed through feedback from others. Embrace constructive criticism, reflect on it, and use it to strengthen yourself. The more you understand yourself, the harder it is for life to knock you off balance.

- **Don't Let Others Dictate Your Worth:** People will try to box you into their own definitions of success, intelligence, and value. But their standards don't matter—yours do. When you know your strengths and weaknesses, you build an unshakable core. No insult, rejection, or failure can shake a person who truly knows themselves.

- **Other People's Opinions Don't Define You, and Neither Does Your Past:** Who you were yesterday is irrelevant to who you can become tomorrow. Your mistakes, failures, and past struggles don't define your future unless you let them. The only opinion that truly matters is the one you hold of yourself. Instead of dwelling on past missteps, use them as stepping stones for growth.

- **The Best Revenge Is Success:** People will doubt you. Some will count you out before you even start. But the most powerful way to silence critics isn't through words—it's through action. Let their doubt fuel your discipline. Turn every weakness into a strength, every failure into a lesson, and every setback into motivation. Nothing stings more than proving them wrong by becoming undeniable.

- **Mastery Is a Choice, not a Talent:** No one is born great at anything. The difference between those who succeed and those who don't isn't luck, it's persistence. Anyone can learn and master a skill with time, effort, and the right mindset. Be a sponge. Absorb knowledge from every source: books, mentors, and life experiences. Observe, learn, and refine your craft every single day. Consistency beats raw talent every time.

- **Your Mindset Shapes Your Reality:** The way you see yourself determines how far you go. If you believe you're capable, you'll take action. If you think you're stuck, you will be. The secret to success isn't external, it's in rewiring your mind to push past self-doubt, embrace discomfort, and chase growth relentlessly.

- **Own Your Story, Own Your Power:** You have full control over your narrative. Every hardship, every mistake, every lesson, it's all part of your story. And the moment you stop seeing yourself as a victim and start seeing yourself as the architect of your future, you become unstoppable.

So, there you have it, a few key things to keep in mind as you move forward. Remember that you're capable of amazing things. Self-awareness is a journey, not a destination. It's about constantly learning and growing.

CHAPTER TWO

Enhancing Your Physical Appearance

"Style is a way to say who you are without having to speak."

— **Rachel Zoe**

Imagine running into your nursery classmate 15 years later. It sounds like something from a movie, right?

Life's unpredictable. Just when you think you've got it figured out, it throws a curveball. For me, that unexpected twist came from meeting someone I had previously encountered, yet I couldn't recall any specific details about them.

At the time, my mom was battling colon cancer, and things had taken a turn for the worse. The doctors said it had spread to her lungs. I met her the day after we found out that terrible news.

I was at a friend's party. Nothing fancy, just a casual get-together outdoors.

And that's when I saw her. She was gorgeous, with a warm smile. Fit, but not too skinny. Exactly my type.

I asked my friend for her number, and soon enough, we started talking. She was studying in an all-girls school in the heart of the city and was from a well-off family. We met up after one of her classes at a coffee shop near her condo, just to hang out.

We clicked instantly same taste in movies, music, everything. But the real shock? We'd met before.

We were nursery classmates: same school, same teacher, same class photo. We even found an old picture of us together.

It feels like everything is meant to happen. Like the universe had put her in my path right when I needed it most. She met me at a strange time in my life, my mom and I were going through such a painful time, and I was so vulnerable then.

I felt she was the one. I'd finally found the girl of my dreams, not because of her physical appearance, but more of what I felt, the connection we had. It was surreal.

But here's the catch. Her family didn't like me.

Her family was wealthy, and compared to me and my mom, we had very little. Her younger sister wasn't fond of me, and even her father, understandably protective of his daughter, was hesitant.

But her mother had grander plans, looking for a suitor who was more well-off and, well, let's just say, more conventionally attractive.

Compared to them, I had no wealth to offer, only my genuine affection for their daughter. We came from different worlds, and the differences clearly showed.

Admittedly, I felt insecure at times, but that didn't stop me from loving her with everything I had.

Then, one day, a friend pulled me aside. He told me something that shattered my world. She'd lied to me about something important, and it made me question if the relationship was worth saving or not.

I felt betrayed, like I'd been made a fool. Looking back now, maybe I was too quick to judge. But at that age, with my heart on my sleeve, it was enough to make me walk away. It hurt like hell, but I had to move on.

I was 18 when I met her. Our romance lasted 90 days.

And like any painful breakup, I turned that pain into fuel. Instead of moping around, I threw myself into something productive. Instead of wallowing in pain, I started consistently going to the gym.

I'd been working out before, but this time, it was different. I was serious about it.

The way I see it, I think I understand why I let that relationship go so easily. It wasn't that I didn't love her; I did. But my ego and insecurities were too much. They were eating me alive. She came from money, her family had everything. Me? I had nothing to my name—nothing that I could be proud of.

Damn pride and insecurity got in the way.

I hit the gym religiously, 6-7 times a week. I was on a mission to get in shape, so I started doing some caloric deficit, started watching what I ate, eating 30 egg whites a day with one whole steamed chicken. I got thinner, leaner, and more ripped, in just a couple of months.

This became my routine, for 3 months. Gym, clean eating, and even facials. I was taking care of myself, and it felt good. My confidence was coming back.

But I still had to deal with the heartbreak. So, on the side, I'd listen to the music we used to love and go to the places we'd been together. It was like exposure therapy, in a way, it was for me to get immune to the memory of her.

I wanted to prove to her family, especially her mom, that I am much more than what they see in me. Yes, I was doing it for myself, self-love, but I wanted to prove the doubters wrong. I wanted to prove them wrong.

Funny how life works, you turn your pain into power, and eventually good things start happening.

I was at the gym doing my usual workout when a man approached me and asked me if I would be interested in doing a VTR. He handed his calling card to me and mentioned that I would be a perfect fit for a print ad project.

I was shocked and excited. Hell yeah! Of course, I accepted. It was my first real modeling gig, a print ad for a huge telecom company, billboard-sized to be exact.

That was the launch pad for my modeling career. I started getting booked for fashion shows, print ads, and commercials, I was even getting booked as an acting support alongside famous Filipino actors and actresses.

So, that's what happened. And the girl? We met again after several years, when my mom passed away. She came to the wake with her boyfriend. But by then, the feelings were long gone.

Thinking about it now, that whole experience taught me a lot about the importance of self-improvement. It's not just about looking good; it's about feeling good about yourself and projecting confidence. That's when people really take notice.

Looking good isn't just about looks. It's about how you carry yourself and how you exude confidence. When you feel good, you project that energy, and people pick up on it. It's like putting on your gym clothes first thing in the morning — it sets the tone for the day and gets you in the right mindset. The same goes for power dressing: you put on that power suit, and you feel like a million bucks!!

If you're going through the same situation as I did, here's what I'd tell you: embrace it. Challenges are what make our lives exciting.

When you're experiencing something painful, acknowledge it. Do not invalidate your feelings. Don't pretend it's not happening. Feel those feelings, let yourself grieve, be angry, or whatever it is. But afterward, pick yourself up.

You could be sad for a day, or two, or maybe at most a week. But after you've given yourself time to feel it all, you must pick yourself back up. Dust yourself off and start rebuilding.

Use that misfortune as a guide and as an opportunity for you to achieve greater things in life. Instead of focusing on what went wrong, focus on what you can do to improve.

Confidence is how you handle setbacks. Life will throw challenges at you, and when it does, you have two choices: let them break you or use them as fuel to level up.

The Dark Horse Mindset isn't about ignoring pain or pretending everything is fine. It's about acknowledging the struggle, feeling it, and then deciding to push forward anyway.

How you see yourself matters. If you project confidence, others will pick up on that. Your mindset shapes how the world sees you. If you carry yourself like you belong at the top, people will start to believe it too.

KEY TAKEAWAYS

Here are some things you can start doing today to feel good, look good, and unleash that inner dark horse:

- **First Impressions Matter**: The way you present yourself is the first thing that people notice. A sharp, well-groomed look signals confidence, self-respect, and discipline. It can open doors, create opportunities, and set the tone for how others perceive you. Whether you like it or not, your appearance speaks before you do, so make it count.

- **Grooming Is Nonnegotiable:** Take care of the basics, get regular haircuts, keep your nails trimmed, clean your ears, pluck excess nose hair, and stay fresh. These small habits separate those who take themselves seriously from those who don't.

- **Confidence Starts with Self-Care:** When you look good, you feel good. Simple things like dressing well, having good posture, and maintaining personal hygiene can boost your confidence instantly. Show up as your best self and take pride in your appearance.

- **Pain Can Be Fuel for Growth:** Rejection, heartbreak, or setbacks can break you or push you to level up. Use tough times as motivation to work on yourself mentally, physically, and emotionally. Instead of dwelling on what went wrong, channel that pain into self-improvement. Hit the gym, learn a new skill, or double down on your goals. Growth happens when you use adversity as motivation.

- **Your Body Is Your Armor:** Strengthen it. A weak body leads to a weak mind. Exercise regularly, eat right, and stay active. Whether it's lifting weights, practicing yoga, or simply moving more, your body will thank you. Looking strong isn't just for aesthetics; it affects how you carry yourself and how others perceive you.

- **Treat Yourself Like You Deserve It:** Buy that shirt, book that massage, and invest in quality grooming products. Small indulgences can elevate your confidence and reinforce the idea that you are worth the effort. When you treat yourself well, others follow suit.

- **Mindset Shapes Reality:** Confidence isn't just about looks; it's about how you own your worth. If you believe you're valuable, others will too. Walk with certainty, speak with conviction, and trust that you belong in any room you enter.

- **Rejection Is Redirection:** Don't let other people's opinions define you. Instead, let them fuel your self-improvement journey. Every "no" is a step closer to the right "yes." The best way to prove doubters wrong is to become undeniable.

- **Success Comes from Consistency:** Whether it's fitness, grooming, or personal growth, showing up daily and putting in the work is what leads to transformation. Quick fixes don't last; consistency does.

- **The Dark Horse Mindset Is Owning Your Power:** It's not about where you come from but how you carry yourself. When you believe in your potential, you become unstoppable. True confidence comes from knowing you are always improving, always growing, and always moving forward.

It takes time to build a habit but stick with it. Whether it's 14, 21, or 66 days, your brain will eventually catch on and realize, "Hey, I can do this!" Trust me, once you've got that momentum, the sky's the limit.

CHAPTER THREE

Mental Fortitude

"It's only after we've lost everything that we're free to do anything." — **Tyler Durden, Fight Club**

What do you do when everything you've worked for disappears overnight?

For many, 2020 changed everything. At first, I saw it as an unplanned vacation, a few weeks off for golf and hobbies. But no one saw what was coming. No one knew how bad it would get.

Suddenly, the news was flooded with rising death tolls. Cities shut down, panic buying emptied the shelves, and face masks became as essential as food. We went from joking about COVID-19 to living under strict lockdowns. No one could leave unless it was for essentials. Businesses closed.

People lost jobs. The world felt dark, and we were all caught in its midst.

If the pandemic taught me anything, it's that no one is invincible. Life will knock you down, no matter how secure you think you are. But this pain gave me perspective. Just like the world had to pause and rethink its priorities, so did I, and I realized that pain isn't just there to hurt you; it forces you to stop, assess, and create another plan of action.

The question is: How do you respond? Do you let it break you, or do you use it to rebuild stronger?

At the time, my businesses and partnerships were slipping away. My personal life was falling apart too.

You see, I had engaged in a business with two of my friends way back in 2019. That was before the pandemic. The business had been thriving for 13 years, and they brought me in to take their marketing to the next level. It was a solid venture, and I was hopeful it would thrive even more.

When we got deeper into the pandemic, our business was affected. A lot of our franchisees bailed, and things got tough. But my biggest issue wasn't the financial loss; it was being dismissed. I had ideas that could help, but my partners wouldn't listen.

In fact, I understood why they were hesitant because a business that has been running for 13 years would think they had it all figured out. I'd come on board to contribute something fresh, but my friends thought they were better off doing it their old ways.

Plus, I started noticing my responsibilities piling up. It wasn't just marketing anymore; I was taking on tasks far beyond my role. Don't get me wrong, I'm no stranger to hard work, and I was fully invested in the company's success. But what weighed on me the most wasn't the workload; it was the realization that we didn't see eye to eye on the things that truly mattered.

Our values were simply not aligned.

So, I decided to cut my losses. I told them I was out.

However, they didn't take it well. Instead of understanding my reasons, they assumed I was bailing just because sales were down.

They started spreading rumors about me, and later, I discovered they had confided in a close friend about their big plans for the business, plans I wasn't even aware of.

That was the final straw. I was done with them. I wanted to distance myself and move on. For me, it wasn't about the money, it was about the principle and the integrity of our relationship.

Sometimes, the hardest decision is knowing when to let go. You can't keep pouring into something that drains you. Whether it's a relationship, a job, or a partnership, if it's taking more than it's giving, it's time to move on.

At the same time, my other businesses began failing. I held on for as long as I could, thinking the pandemic would pass quickly. I kept paying my staff, covering expenses, and hoping for the best.

But the reality was brutal. I was losing money left and right. The real estate market? Dead. My production studio? It had to go. That one hurt the most because I'd put a lot of heart and money into this business. Packing up my gear felt like giving up a part of myself.

And then, COVID hit my family. My wife and mother-in-law got sick.

It felt like the whole world was crashing down on me.

I lay on the sofa, staring at the ceiling. In my entire life, I'd only cried three times: when my mom died, when my son was born, and now.

For a few days, I was like this. Didn't leave the room, and barely spoke to anyone, not even to my wife or the kids. I just wanted to shut the world out and wallow in my misery. I'd replay the problems over and over in my head, but no solutions came. I was paralyzed, lost, and drifting away.

"How do I start over?" I'd ask myself. "How do I bounce back from this kind of mess? What the hell am I going to do?"

I was a wreck, physically and mentally. I wasn't eating right and hadn't shaved in days. I didn't even care about how I looked anymore. What was the point? I felt (and looked) like a castaway, stranded on a deserted island.

Sometimes, I questioned God. Why me? I wasn't a bad person, so why did this always happen to me? Is this some kind of punishment for being too trusting, too generous? Does the world hate goodness so much that it has to destroy it?

When life stops making sense, you search for answers. Anything to justify what's happening.

But now, I see it for what it was: a redirection. A necessary shift toward something greater.

There's a saying in the Philippines, "Kung kailan ka bibigay, dun ibibigay" which means, "Just when you're about to break, that's when the breakthrough happens." That's exactly why I chose Tyler Durden's line for this chapter: "It's only after we've lost everything that we're free to do anything." At my lowest point, empty, lost, and stripped of control, I had two choices: fight circumstances that I couldn't change or surrender to the process. I chose to let go and trust that there was something bigger at play.

I had no control over these circumstances, but I could control how I reacted to them.

When you're finally ready to let go, to accept things as they are, that's when you're truly free. You've got nothing left to lose, so you're not afraid to take risks, to rebuild, to become a better version of yourself.

When you do that, that's when life opens new doors and shows you a different path.

So, when I finally hit that point, when I was ready to face all the crap that had happened, that's when a new opportunity presented itself.

You see, my wife was desperate to help me. I wasn't talking to her, I wasn't even listening to anyone, just me and those dark thoughts swirling in my head. She figured maybe a professional could get through to me.

One day, she was scrolling through Instagram, and two people popped up on her feed: a Reiki healer and a hypnotherapist. It was strange, but something told her she needed to reach out to the hypnotherapist.

But when she suggested it, I said no. I didn't want some stranger poking around in my head, digging up all my deepest, darkest secrets. I was skeptical, but at that point, what did I have to lose? So, I gave it some thought, went online and did some research, and eventually, gave it a shot.

And hypnotherapy doesn't work like how it's portrayed in the movies, you know, with the swinging watch and all that. Hypnotherapy helps you reset and get your thoughts in order.

The way it works is it's just you and the hypnotherapist, talking one-on-one. You tell your story, and they ask you some questions to get you thinking about things differently.

I remember during my session when the hypnotherapist had me imagine three doors. I opened one, and she asked me what I saw. I saw my younger self. She asked what I'd say to him. I hugged him and told him not to be so hard on himself, that everything was gonna be alright.

And you know what? It worked. Hypnotherapy helped me deal with all the shit I was going through. It helped me develop a stronger mental fortitude and become better at coping with adversity because I was finally able to understand myself on a deeper level.

For example, I've always had this tendency to go above and beyond for the people I love, even if it's inconvenient or uncomfortable for me. If I care about someone, I'll do anything to help them. I realize this pattern stems from my childhood experiences. Growing up alone at 10, then lost my mom when I was 21, it's like I always wanted to be the kind of person I didn't have back then, the one who'd be there for others no matter what. It was my inner child speaking, trying to fill a void.

Hypnotherapy helped me recognize my own habits and patterns, trace them back to their origins, and finally understand why I did the things I did. And once I saw it, I could do something about it.

Like my obsession with buying shoes.

When I was a kid, my mom could only afford to buy me one pair of shoes a year. I remember when my old pair broke, I asked her if I could get a pair of Jordan 11 Breds. Those shoes meant everything to me at the time. But she couldn't afford them.

That didn't stop me, though.

I had a friend who had a pair, so I asked if I could borrow them. There was just one problem, his shoe size was 8.5, and mine was 9.5.

Did that stop me? Nope.

I forced my feet into those shoes, ignored the pain, and wore them like they were mine. And yeah, I looked fresh for a day, but when I took them off, my toenails were dead. Black and blue. It was a painful reminder that forcing something that isn't meant for you always comes with a cost.

I didn't realize it then, but that moment stuck with me. And without even knowing it, I carried it into adulthood. I became obsessed with buying shoes, not because I needed them, but because deep down, I was still that kid trying to get the things that he once couldn't afford.

This is why understanding your past is so important. Because if you don't, you'll keep repeating patterns you don't even realize you're trapped in.

A lot of people walk through life stuck in cycles they don't even know exist. They keep making the same mistakes, attracting the same toxic relationships, or holding themselves back without knowing why. If you don't take the time to understand yourself, your triggers, your tendencies, and your motivations, then you're not in control. Your past is.

And if you let your past run the show, you'll keep ending up in the same place, repeatedly.

Mental fortitude means knowing yourself so well that nothing controls you, not your past, not your fears, not other people. That's the real strength.

Once I started feeling good, everything else started falling into place. When the pandemic eased up a bit, this big company called me for a project. And then another one, and another one. It was like a domino effect, one good thing leading to another.

Everything was shifting, this new positive energy was flowing, and suddenly everything started to feel right.

And get this: remember that business venture I lost during the pandemic? It turns out that I lost one but gained two more after that.

When the projects started rolling in, I got in touch with a colleague and thought, why not start an advertising agency? That way, I could offer not just the production side, but the whole ad package. So, I did! Our ad agency (AYO Creatives) was one of my businesses that stemmed from the pandemic.

I also thought of creating my own podcast. So, I started this mini-series Coledale "Pop" The first episode was just a 5-minute vlog about trails, and it got around 200 shares. It was a decent start, but it was a lot of work, and it wasn't taking off as quickly as I'd hoped.

During one of my projects, my cinematographer introduced me to a technical director. At first, our relationship was strictly business, but after a few conversations, I realized that we shared the same drive and passion, and we just clicked. As we talked more about life, I saw how much this guy had to offer. Curious, I checked out his social media and found out he had a podcast, although it wasn't getting much traction.

That's when I asked him if he was interested in doing a podcast with me and he agreed. We called it, "Life Over Whiskey." The name came from the fact that I love talking about life with friends over a glass of whiskey. The whole point was to share real, authentic stories, and to give people something valuable they could connect with.

Today, our podcast has over 600k followers, and we've collaborated with hundreds of amazing people who share our mission. It's been an incredible journey, and it all started with that one moment of self-discovery.

Looking back, whatever I have now, I earned it. It wasn't handed to me on a silver platter. Even when I was at rock bottom, I never stooped to anything shady to get ahead. No backstabbing, no cutting corners. Just grit, hard work, and perseverance. I wasn't even the most talented guy out there; I just kept pushing myself to get better.

I always tell people that integrity matters. Do the right thing, even when no one's watching. Trust me, it makes a difference. When you live your life with integrity, good things happen.

The toughest moments in life can lead to the greatest breakthroughs. When you hit rock bottom, you have no choice but to look inward, to confront your deepest fears and insecurities. And in that process, you discover a strength you never knew you had. You learn to turn pain into power, to rise above the occasion, and to emerge as a stronger, more resilient version of yourself.

That's the essence of the Dark Horse Mindset. It's not about being perfect or having all the answers. It's about embracing your flaws, learning from your mistakes, and never giving up, no matter how many times life knocks you down.

That's why I believe that anyone who's resilient can achieve anything. It's how the mind and the universe work. It's like food—you are what you eat. The same goes for your thoughts. If you feed your mind with positivity, if you believe you're capable of great things, the universe will find a way to make it happen.

But here's the challenge, you also need to act. Positive thinking is great, but it's not enough. You got to put in the work. Don't wait for the perfect moment, just start now. Do it now because the world's not gonna wait for you.

You may feel like the odds are stacked against you. You may feel broken, betrayed, and beaten down. But you are more powerful than you know. Your pain is not your prison; it's your platform.

When you're stripped of everything, you discover the essence of who you are. And it's in that essence, your raw, unfiltered self, that you find your greatest strength.

So, lean into the discomfort. Confront your fears. Let the world doubt you but never doubt yourself. Turn your pain into power and rise as the dark horse that no one saw coming.

KEY TAKEAWAYS

We've talked about mental toughness, turning pain into power, but how do you put this into practice? How do you go from simply understanding resilience to living it? Here are a few things you can start doing today to build that unbreakable spirit:

- **Prayer:** I am not the one to preach and as cheesy as it may sound, this works for me, Prayer isn't just about asking for things but grounding yourself, finding peace in chaos, and reminding yourself that you're not alone. And if you're not religious, that's fine too. What matters is finding something greater than yourself to lean on, whether it's faith, the universe, or even just believing in your own purpose. Because when life gets hard, having something to hold onto makes all the difference.

- **Meditation:** This helps you chill out, focus your mind, and deal with stress, like a mental workout. Think of meditation as weightlifting for your brain. When you lift weights, you tear your muscles down so they can grow back stronger. Meditation does the same thing for your mind. It forces you to slow down, focus, and sit with your thoughts instead of running from them. At first, it's uncomfortable. Your mind races. You feel restless. But over time? You build mental endurance. You train yourself to stay calm under pressure, to let go of stress instead of letting it consume you. And just like lifting weights, consistency is key. Even five minutes a day can make a huge difference.

- **Accept What You Cannot Change:** Life's challenges often come with an emotional weight we resist carrying. But resistance doesn't solve problems; acceptance does. Acknowledge your pain, name it, and release the burden of control. For example, I couldn't change my past. I couldn't change growing up alone, losing my mom, or the struggles I faced. But I could change how I let those experiences define me. Instead of letting them break me, I let them shape me. "I can't change the pandemic, but I can change how I adapt to it."

- **Reframe Your Struggles:** Challenges are not punishments; they are lessons. Your struggles are your greatest teachers. Instead of asking, "Why is this happening to me?" ask, "What is this teaching me?" The most profound growth often comes from our most painful experiences. Every painful experience I've had, every loss, every failure, and every tough moment, has made me stronger, smarter, and sharper. I wouldn't be who I am today without them. So, when you face hardships, remember that they aren't here to break you; they're here to build you.

- **Seek Guidance and Support:** You don't have to do everything alone. One of the biggest shifts in my life happened when I got help. For me, it was hypnotherapy. Not because I was "broken" or needed "fixing," but because I needed a new perspective. Whether it's therapy, a mentor, or even just talking to someone who's been where you are, don't be afraid to seek help. There's power in learning from those who have walked the path before you.

- **Establish Small Routines for Big Gains:** Most people think transformation happens overnight. It doesn't. It happens in the small, daily habits that seem insignificant but add up over time. So, begin with tiny, consistent actions that rebuild your foundation. For me, it started with simple things, working out, meditating, and eating right again. These small victories snowball into larger shifts.

- **Set Boundaries and Reclaim Your Energy:** Not everyone deserves your time. Not every battle is worth fighting. One of the hardest but most powerful lessons I've learned is to protect my energy. Pain has a way of teaching you who truly has your back. And when you start valuing yourself, you realize that some people, some situations, and some habits are just not worth your peace. Learn to say no. Walk away when something isn't serving you. You don't have to set yourself on fire to keep others warm.

Train your mind like you train your body. Building mental fortitude is like training for a marathon.

You must put in the miles. You must push through the pain. You must stay committed, even when it's hard.

It takes time and effort.

But here's what I can promise you: When you develop that unbreakable mindset, there is NOTHING life can throw at you that you won't overcome. Your past doesn't define you. Your pain doesn't control you. You are stronger than you think.

And the sooner you believe that? The sooner you start becoming unstoppable.

CHAPTER FOUR

Humility

"You are the same decaying organic matter as everything else."
— **Tyler Durden, Fight Club**

By now, you're probably wondering why all my quotes are from *Fight Club*.

Well, here's the thing: this movie changed me in more ways than I can count.

It came out in 1999, but I didn't watch it until 2000. The movie's plot was fresh; it was one of those mindfuck movies. For those who haven't watched it, I insist you do. Just for the context of this chapter, I'll give you a brief overview. It's about the Narrator (Edward Norton) and how his life turned upside down when he let his alter ego, Tyler Durden (Brad Pitt) takes over.

The twist is unexpected, but here's what I took away: we all have an alter ego or even multiple personalities. Edward Norton wouldn't have achieved great success if it wasn't for his alter ego, Tyler Durden. So, the same with life. We have altered egos that help us deal with adversities. Every person is wearing multiple hats, and that makes you create different personalities for each of those hats. For example, how I treat my colleagues at work is different from when I'm at home; whereas I'm different as a colleague and I'm an entirely different person as a father and a husband.

There are so many golden nuggets in that movie, but one of the big reasons why I love it so much is that it's a movie about self-awareness and that you don't have to conform to the norm if it means leaving your authentic self. My life revolves around Fight Club. I feel like even my artistic side was ignited because of that movie.

Back to the quote: this was one of the most valuable lessons I took from the movie, and it played a huge role in my success. It doesn't matter if you're a CEO or a janitor; at the end of the day, we all end up in the same place, and you can't take your title with you. This is what humility means, learning how to deal with people from all walks of life. If you know how to master this art, then trust me, you'll go a long way, and I can attest to that too.

Growing up, my mom worked long hours to raise me alone, so I spent a lot of time on my own. I would often go out and play with the kids in our area. These kids weren't well-off. They were children of low-income earners. Now I told you that my mom and I weren't rich, even if she came from a rich clan, but we weren't that deprived either, we were living just about right. So, there was a difference economically between the kids and me, but I didn't really think much about that, as I was young and all I knew back then was that I wanted to play with kids my age. We played basketball barefoot, ate together, and drank ice tubig (tap water in plastic bags that you could buy from sari-sari stores). We would sometimes even make a bet, and the winner would get a pop cola from the loser.

My mom noticed who I was hanging out with and told me to choose my friends wisely because they were a reflection of who I was. At first, I thought she was just judgmental since she didn't really know them, but when I grew older, I kind of understood what my mom meant.

But by then, it was already part of who I was. I didn't really care much about who you were and where you came from. As long you and I treat each other with respect, then we're good.

I loved hanging out with those kids, but thinking about it now, I realize maybe the reason why I loved hanging out with them was I felt the connection, the relatability of how people like them are always being seen as small. Just like the same feeling I have with my rich relatives, how I felt small compared to them.

But at the same time, I feel like the universe is preparing me for something else, telling me not to be those people who judge other people.

I carried those values with me until now. How I treat CEOs and prominent clients of mine are how I also treat janitors and other people.

When your core values guide your actions, life tends to fall into place.

You won't always get help from the people you expect, but that doesn't mean help won't come. The universe has a way of rewarding those who give without expecting anything in return. Call it good karma, call it energy, whatever it is, it works.

I've had moments where I helped someone without thinking twice, and later, when I needed a hand, the right person showed up, sometimes a stranger, sometimes an unexpected connection. But that's the power of putting good out into the world. It doesn't always come back from the same source, but it always finds its way back to you, often in ways bigger than you imagined.

That's where humility comes in, it strengthens trust, deepens relationships, and opens doors in ways that ego never could. A humble attitude attracts people because it signals authenticity. And when relationships are built on authenticity and respect, they hold far more value than those based purely on personal gain.

Humility also creates space for self-awareness and growth. I learned this the hard way. When I was a model, I felt on top of the world, fame and fortune came early. But life has a way of keeping you in check. After my mom passed, everything changed.

And even though I wanted to stay in that lane in the hopes of becoming an actor someday, I took a step back and assessed. I was getting old, and it was getting tougher to get booked, so I needed a plan for a steadier income, which then led me to try real estate. And I have no regrets, because the amount I got from doing modeling tripled in my role as the top director for this real estate company.

You see, being humble also means acknowledging that you don't have all the answers, and that's okay! Because it then fosters a mindset of learning over your ego. Dark horses often succeed, not because they know everything, but because they are willing to identify weaknesses and improve them.

Another great thing about humility is that It enhances your leadership in ways you cannot imagine. You see, I've been a consistent leading director for our real estate company, and one trait that separates me from the others is my leadership skills.

As the leader of my team, I make sure to guide them, not just in terms of work, but I ask them how they are in their personal lives.

How did you spend your weekend? Did you go to the gym today? What's your purpose in life? If people feel that they're being valued, seen, and cared for, they are always willing to go the extra mile for you.

And the results speak for themselves. I see it in my team's productivity, their dedication, and the energy they bring to work every day. They're not just showing up, they're inspired, engaged, and fully invested in what they do. That kind of energy is contagious.

Some of my co-directors don't get my leadership style. They think I get too attached to my team. My response? It's a double-edged sword, but it's also why my team consistently performs at the top. Building real connections fosters loyalty, and that loyalty translates to results. Is it always perfect? No. There are times when people question my intentions, assuming I'm putting on a facade just to be liked. But you can't control everything. At the end of the day, I trust my instincts; if it feels right, it usually is.

I also believe in leading by example. If I expect my people to be early, sharp, and professional, I make sure I'm the first one at the office, looking the part. Leadership isn't about commanding. It's about setting the standard. Walk the talk.

This is where the Dark Horse Mindset comes in, those who lead by example rather than authority. A humble approach to dealing with different individuals is the type of servant leadership, where your influence is built through action and respect rather than control or fear. Dark horses lift others up, recognizing the power of empowering people, regardless of their background or status.

Be genuine, be kind, but most of all, keep on doing good deeds but at the same time stay humble despite the success. Humility keeps you grounded and reminds you that one's self-worth isn't tied to external validation but to the way you treat others, no matter who they are.

In the end, dealing with people from all walks of life teaches you the same thing, that your worth isn't in what you own or how others see you. It's in the respect, kindness, and authenticity you bring to everyone you meet, whether it's with someone in the gym, a CEO, or a janitor.

When you stay humble and treat everyone with the same level of care, you stop being owned by ego or possessions, and that's when you really start to grow.

KEY TAKEAWAYS/ACTION

Humility is a quiet strength that builds trust, fosters meaningful connections, and shapes the way you interact with the world. Here's how you can embody humility in your daily life:

- **Humility Strengthens Relationships:** Humility builds trust and deeper connections. It attracts authentic relationships that hold more value than ones based on personal gain. When you approach people with humility, you remove barriers to connection. You become approachable, relatable, and trustworthy. It's about recognizing that every person you meet has something to teach you. It allows you to listen more than you speak, admit when you're wrong, and appreciate the perspectives of others. This mindset naturally attracts people who value honesty and authenticity, creating relationships based on mutual respect rather than self-interest. Change made: So, the next time you're in a conversation, actively listen without thinking about your response. Give people the space to share their thoughts and experiences.
- **Shaping Your Values and Morals:** Your core values dictate how you treat others. When you stay true to strong moral principles, like respect, kindness, and fairness, you naturally build meaningful relationships and gain respect in return. Success isn't just about

what you achieve but also about the impact you have on others. Humility ensures that your actions align with your values, no matter where life takes you.

- **Never Judge a Person:** Wealth, status, or background doesn't define a person's worth. Everyone has a story, and you never know their struggles. True humility comes from acknowledging that no one is inherently above or beneath you. The next time you find yourself making a judgment, pause and ask, "Do I really know this person's story?" Challenge yourself to approach them with curiosity rather than assumption.

- **Be Open-Minded:** Approaching life with an open mind allows you to learn from different people, perspectives, and experiences. Set aside your ego and listen, and you'll gain wisdom from unexpected places. The most successful and fulfilled people aren't those who think they know everything, but those who are willing to learn from everyone. Humility helps you set aside your ego, listen to different perspectives, and embrace new ideas. It allows you to accept that you don't have all the answers, and that's okay. Seek out conversations with people who have different perspectives. Instead of debating, focus on understanding. Ask questions and be willing to change your mind.

- **Have Genuine Intentions Toward People:** People can sense authenticity. When you interact with others, do so with sincerity, not because of what they can do for you, but because you genuinely care. Perform one selfless act today without expecting anything in return. Compliment someone, offer help, or simply check in on a friend.

- **Keep Doing Good, Because the Energy You Give Is the Energy You Receive:** The world operates on energy; what you put out, you get back. If you treat people with kindness, honesty, and humility, life has a way of returning that energy to you in unexpected ways. Even if it feels like no one is noticing your efforts, keep doing good. The impact you make often unfolds over time; in ways you may never even realize. So, make giving a habit. Whether it's your time, kindness, or resources, contribute to the world without looking for immediate rewards.

- **Walk the Talk:** People follow those who inspire them, not those who demand respect without earning it. Lead by example. The best leaders don't just talk; they show how it's done. Identify one area in your life where your actions don't fully align with your words. Commit to changing that today.

By applying these principles in your daily life, you'll build stronger relationships, gain respect effortlessly, and leave a lasting impact on the people around you.

PART TWO

CULTIVATING RELATIONSHIPS

CHAPTER FIVE

Effective Communication

"If I didn't say anything, people always assume the worst."

— The Narrator, Fight Club

We've now reached the second part of the book. The first four chapters laid the foundation for building confidence, developing self-awareness, and becoming the best version of yourself.

But success isn't just about what you can do; it's about the relationships you build, and that's what this second part will teach you.

No one succeeds alone. In fact, a big percentage of my success came from referrals and past relationships. Connections built not on transactions but on mutual trust and respect.

This is the reality of any career. The most successful people aren't just the smartest or the hardest working; they're the ones who understand people. They cultivate trust, foster strong relationships, and communicate in a way that aligns with their values.

When your words align with your values and intentions, you create deeper, more meaningful relationships based on trust and respect.

I see this play out all the time in real estate. I never overpromise but I always overdeliver. When I talk to potential buyers, I make sure to communicate the turnover date and its deliverables and never go beyond that. I often see agents trying to overpromise just to close the deal, but the buyers end up being disappointed when they see the unit, and it's not what they expected or was communicated to them.

Back in 2011, when we started marketing this residential project, we were upfront with clients about what to expect. We were very transparent; the tiles and walls will be painted white, so their expectation is just that. But when we delivered the units, the clients were surprised to see they already had lights and even an air conditioner.

For creative projects, I outline the hours my team and I will work and the cost for revisions in the contract. I make sure I properly communicate this to my clients. But sometimes I go beyond that. During the shoot, I make sure to finish what needs to be done, regardless of the hours and revisions. If I know that these clients really believed in my creative vision, I will sometimes waive the additional revision fee. I would also help them market the video that I made for them, even to the extent of patronizing their product.

Never overpromise. Always be transparent. And if you're going to surprise someone, do it by giving them more than they expect, not less. Integrity isn't just about doing what's right, it's about building trust, earning loyalty, and setting a standard so high that people can't help but respect you.

The way I bring this value to my team is different.

I may be their boss, but I treat my team like family. I care that they achieve their goals because I see it as a reflection of my leadership. I had a team member who struggled with confidence and sales. He was an introvert, and closing deals didn't come naturally to him. I asked him, "What's your goal in life?" He said he wanted to go to Australia cause that's where his family is. So, I told him, if you want something, you should get it, no matter what. If you want something, go after it—now. If you have no resources to do it, then create those resources. I told him if he's able to make several sales within the year, then that dream of his will be within his reach.

As a leader, I also make sure to track their progress. For example, when I ask them "What's your purpose and goal?" some of them would say to travel, to take their parents out of the country, to establish a business, then I would always track their progress since I know how much their commissions are. I would ask them: "How far are we in the business? What stage are you now in your Hong Kong travel goal?" I don't want to take credit, of course, but my people tell me that I make the office a place of growth and comfort for them.

I have this team member who before was not really under my wing. In fact, she was my competitor; we were both eyeing the same position. When I got the promotion, we stayed friends still. However, something happened to her at work which led to her almost getting laid off from the company. I offered her to stay on my team so she could still retain her job. And you know what? It was the best decision she made because now she has her own 11M house, 3 brand-new cars, and a new business. Now, she is an executive sales manager and no longer a sales agent. She is even the top seller in my team.

People follow those who inspire them, not those who demand respect without earning it. Lead by example. The best leaders don't just talk; they show how it's done. Identify one area in your life where your actions don't fully align with your words and commit to changing that today.

But sometimes, leadership isn't about helping someone win a promotion or achieve financial success. Sometimes, it's about navigating the unexpected, about finding strength when life doesn't go according to plan.

And that's exactly what happened to me when I became a father.

I remember the moment everything changed. My wife was a few weeks pregnant when the doctors found markers for Down syndrome. Still, they gave us hope and told us there was still a chance our son might not have Down syndrome. And so, I held on to that. I convinced myself that everything would be "normal."

Then the day came in the delivery room.

I saw my boy... but my heart sank.

I cried, it was tears of joy, but also it was sadness and confusion all together.

My son did have Down syndrome.

And the crushing realization that the life I'd imagined for my son, for myself, was gone.

I had dreams and expectations for him, but all of that was gone now. I didn't know how to cope with something like this.

I had to confront a truth I wasn't prepared for, that my son's journey was not going to be the one I had scripted.

And that scared the shit out of me.

But in the midst of all that uncertainty, something powerful happened. People showed up. People who were in the same community reached out and assured us that things would be okay. That there was a reason for all of this.

And they were right. Because as my son grew, I witnessed something extraordinary, he was a better version of me. Kinder, more loving, more pure-hearted. He didn't need to be better at sports. He didn't need to be a reflection of my own expectations. He was simply himself, and that was enough.

Remember that I used to be a model? Well, so was my son. In 2018, he became the face of World Down Syndrome Day in the Philippines.

Imagine if my son had been born to a family without love, without patience, without the means to support him, what would have happened to him? But he was given to us. And that meant something.

I recently shared my son's story on my podcast, "Life Over Whiskey." I didn't pretend to have it all together. I didn't try to sugarcoat my fears. I spoke openly about my doubts, my struggles, and my growth. In just 36 hours, that reel exploded with 2 million views. But it wasn't because of clever editing or a perfect script. It was because, for once, I allowed myself to be completely vulnerable. I didn't hold back. I didn't try to be strong. I simply spoke from the heart.

When we are real, when we are vulnerable, when we speak with authenticity, we create real connections.

Parents of children with special needs flooded the comments. "Finally, someone who gets it," they wrote. My story gave them permission to be proud and to embrace their journey without shame. I even remember a person with a disability thanked me, not just for sharing, but for being proud of my son.

So, what's the lesson here?

Effective communication isn't about sounding perfect but it's about being real. It's about saying the things most people are afraid to say, and in doing so, creating a space where others feel safe to be themselves. It's about integrity, sticking to your values, being transparent, and leading with purpose.

People don't connect with perfection. They connect with authenticity. And when you're willing to show up, flaws and all, you don't just inspire people, you change lives.

And how does this tie up with the Dark Horse Mindset?

You can't sell yourself, your brand, your business, or your vision if people don't trust what you say. And people won't trust what you say if your words lack integrity.

This is where so many fail. They focus on looking successful instead of being trustworthy. But the dark horse doesn't need validation. They don't chase approval. Instead, they refine how they communicate, with purpose, with truth, with unwavering moral character.

That's why this chapter is more than just a lesson on communication; it's a lesson on power.

The power of speaking honestly. The power of being real in a world full of masks. The power of selling yourself, not by pretending to be something you're not, but by standing firm in who you truly are.

Because in the end, the dark horse doesn't win by chance. They win because they earned it.

KEY TAKEAWAYS

- **Communicate with Integrity and Transparency:** Never overpromise just to get ahead. Set clear expectations, always deliver, and when possible, overdeliver. Trust is built on honesty. In a world where people often make exaggerated claims to get ahead, integrity and transparency set you apart. Whether in business, friendships, or leadership, honesty is the foundation of trust. Integrity means being upfront about challenges, admitting when you don't have all the answers, and standing by your word. People gravitate toward those they can rely on. The more honest and transparent you are, the stronger your relationships will be.

- **Set Clear Expectations to Manage Emotions:** Most disappointments come from unclear expectations. Whether in business or personal relationships, define expectations early to avoid unnecessary conflict. When expectations are unclear, people fill in the blanks with their own assumptions, which often leads to disappointment. Whether you're leading a team, managing clients, or building relationships, setting expectations from the start prevents misunderstandings. Clearly define what can and cannot be done, outline responsibilities, and ensure that everyone is on the same page. This applies beyond business. Healthy relationships thrive on open conversations about needs and boundaries. Clarity prevents unnecessary emotional stress and fosters smoother interactions. Clarity prevents unnecessary emotional stress and fosters smoother interactions.

- **Give More Than You Take:** The best communicators don't just focus on what they can gain but on how they can provide value. Whether it's an extra service, a thoughtful gesture, or genuine support, people remember those who go the extra mile. In business, it could mean providing exceptional service, offering helpful advice, or making introductions that benefit others. In personal relationships, it could be as simple as listening intently or showing up when someone needs support. People remember those who make their lives better, even in small ways.

- **Use Communication to Empower Others:** True leadership is about helping others succeed. Great leaders don't just instruct; they inspire. Words have the power to elevate, encourage, and instill confidence. Whether you're managing a team, mentoring someone, or simply engaging with peers, your communication should align with their aspirations. When people feel supported and understood, they are more likely to push past their limitations. Instead of just giving feedback, ask how you can help. Instead of pointing out problems, guide people toward solutions. The right words at the right time can unlock someone's full potential, fostering an environment of growth and achievement.

- **Speak with Kindness and Give Credit Where It's Due:** Recognition costs nothing but has the power to transform relationships. Acknowledge people's efforts, as it fuels motivation. A simple "thank you" or "great job" can boost morale and deepen trust. In teams, crediting individuals for their contributions creates a culture of respect and motivation. In personal relationships, acknowledging efforts strengthens bonds. Kindness in communication doesn't mean avoiding difficult conversations; it means delivering them with empathy. Whether offering praise or constructive feedback, the way you speak can either build people up or tear them down. Choose to uplift.

- **Be Vulnerable and Authentic:** Perfection doesn't inspire. Realness does. People connect more with authenticity than perfection. When you share real experiences, including failures, fears, and lessons learned, you create meaningful relationships built on trust. Sharing your struggles, failures, and fears makes you more approachable and trustworthy. Vulnerability isn't a weakness; it's a strength that invites others to do the same. Whether in leadership, friendships, or content creation, authenticity fosters deeper relationships. Being open about your journey, both the wins and the losses, allows others to see themselves in you. It creates an environment where people feel safe to be their true selves.

- **Your Words Have Power, Use Them Wisely:** Words can either build or destroy. Speak with purpose. A careless remark can discourage someone, while an encouraging word can change their life. Whether in casual conversations, negotiations, or leadership, choose your words with intention. Speak with clarity, purpose, and mindfulness. Ask yourself: Will this inspire you? Will this clarify? Will this help? Thoughtful communication fosters trust, motivates action, and leaves a lasting impact. Every conversation is an opportunity to build or destroy. Choose wisely.

CHAPTER SIX

Network Expansion

"Your network is your Net Worth." **— Anonymous**

There's a saying that goes, "You become the company you are with" and I'm a firm believer of this.

The people you surround yourself with will influence your mindset and actions. If you immerse yourself in a group of successful individuals, you'll naturally start adopting their habits and perspectives. You'll know how they think, how they work, and how they interact with people, and eventually, you will even adapt to the kind of life they have.

I started to realize that I wanted to become that type of person when I started working as a salesman for a luxurious car brand. These brands were premium, top of the top. I'll give you a hint at some of the brands I sold: one logo is a horse, another one is a big cat, another is a trident, and the last one has this green circular logo with its brand name (rhymes with clover). This company sold high-end luxury cars that only the top 1% could afford, including business owners, investors, and industry leaders.

As a salesman, I had the opportunity to interact with these high-net-worth individuals, seeing their luxury watches, cars, fashion choices, and even their dining preferences. It gave me a glimpse into their world.

After spending time in real estate, I transitioned into selling luxury cars, a role I held for about three to four years. This gave me the exposure and experience to engage with high-profile clients.

You see, the difference between being a real estate salesman and a luxury car salesman is that in real estate, you approach people to buy houses, which is a necessity, while in selling premium luxury cars, people approach you because only a select few are willing to spend a significant amount on something that is not essential.

This is when I realized I wanted to have this kind of life. Being in this network challenged me but in a good way. I was doubted by my own family and got the judgment already of someone who would not succeed in life, so I wanted to prove them wrong too, that's why I aspired to become like these people.

But here's the thing, I never acted desperate to fit into their world. Instead, I focused on adding value. I carried myself with the same confidence they did, despite knowing I had nothing compared to their wealth. I'm not gonna lie, it is intimidating sometimes, but you want to know the secret of how I did it? I always thought to myself that I could contribute something of value to them. For example, I was a salesman, so I gave value to them by providing the best service, not just by selling cars, no, I also gave advice, business insights, and the like. It wasn't just about the money, because I had none of that, so I offered my skills, my knowledge, and my time.

If you treat them like celebrities, they'll see you as just another fan. But if you treat them as equals, they'll do the same for you.

So, what's my point here? If you want to build a powerful network, you must give value first.

Many thinks networking is just about meeting the right people and collecting contacts. But real connections are built on value. You don't get welcomed into high-level circles; you earn your place by offering something meaningful.

That's exactly what I did. I didn't chase after wealthy clients like a desperate salesman. I positioned myself as someone they could rely on, someone who provided insights, solutions, and an exceptional experience. I didn't have money, status, or a big name to offer, but what I did have was my knowledge, my service, and my ability to make their lives easier. And because of that, these high-value clients started seeing me as more than just a salesman.

Some of them became friends, some became mentors, and some even opened doors for me that I never thought possible.

One of those doors opened when I found myself back in real estate after spending a few years as a car salesman.

I remember it very well because it was November 1, and our boss asked us if somebody was willing to work on that day. For context, November 1 is a holiday in the Philippines and, of course, nobody wanted to work on that day, so I volunteered.

And on that day, a couple walked in and inquired about the project. You could tell based on their looks that they were from high society. Eloquent people with Spanish lineage.

"Hi Sir, how can I help you today?" I asked them.

"Oh hello! We were just looking around because we just went to the other showroom with your competitor."

"Is this your first time, Sir? I'd be more than happy to assist you."

And while we were talking, we clicked suddenly, and we started talking about our hobbies, and interests, while on the side talking about the project.

Then he told me, "You know, I'll be very honest with you, we came here to check the project because you guys are a competitor of the project right across, which is a very popular developer. And you guys are just starting, but you know, we really like you and we're just curious, since you guys are a start-up, what's going to happen to our units if your developer is not able to deliver?"

"Well, Sir, the chances are slim to none because the company is well-funded and is publicly listed. The major stockholder owns the largest canning business in the country and is listed in Forbes wealthiest. If you ask me if the project's gonna fly? Yes, I do believe it will because this is the first LEED-certified residential high-rise in the Philippines."

A few days later, they called back and decided to buy five units. What started as a single interaction turned into something bigger. Because they came from a well-known family in politics and business, they referred nearly all their relatives to us. In total, they bought several units through me, roughly PHP 300 million worth of sales.

And our relationship wasn't just transactional anymore; we developed a friendship. We discovered that we shared the same interests as golf, photography, watches, and cars. There were times that we would hang out to play golf or have conversations about life and our common interests.

Just imagine, out of all the days, they came around at a time when I was manning the office, and it was a holiday too. There was no assurance that I was going to close a sale with them, and there was also no assurance that they would buy from me. But because I showed up and made myself present that day, opportunities were presented, and I was able to grab it.

This story is proof that success in networking isn't just about making a sale; it's about building genuine relationships. I didn't close that deal because I had the best sales pitch. I closed it because I took the time to connect with my clients on a personal level, to understand their concerns, and to be completely honest with them.

Opportunities come when you least expect them, but only if you're prepared and willing to put yourself in the right position. Had I decided to take the holiday off like everyone else, I wouldn't have met this couple. Had I treated them like just another sales prospect instead of people I genuinely wanted to connect with, I wouldn't have built a lasting relationship with them. And because I gave them an experience beyond just a transaction, they didn't just become clients, they became a part of my network and even my friends.

This wasn't the first time my network opened doors for me, and it wasn't the last. In fact, my next big break in business came from an entirely different circle: my wakeboarding crew. Little did I know that my passion for wakeboarding would eventually lead to the creation of Paper St. Production, a business that would change my career path entirely.

You see, in wakeboarding, most of us film ourselves so we'll know how we did a certain trick. I decided to learn about video editing since we were shooting anyway. Then, one of the wakeboarders saw my edits and asked me if I could offer my videography services to one of her clients who was going to have a debut. So, I gave it a shot. This was my first professional work as a videographer, my first portfolio, and then after this, other wakeboarders would also approach me for other videography services for their child's birthday, weddings, and so on.

This paved the way for me to become a professional videographer, and because I grew my portfolio, I also grew my network, until there came a time when big companies would hire me as their videographer, which eventually led me to become a director.

And so, when big companies and big brands were hiring me constantly, I decided it was time to put up a production company that specializes in video and photos, just so I could be official. I built Paper St Production so I could cater to my clients and consider them now as my own.

Building good relationships is an integral part of success. Every major opportunity in my life came from a relationship I built, a connection I nurtured, or a risk I took. If I hadn't taken the time to genuinely connect with my clients, that one sale wouldn't have snowballed into something bigger. If I hadn't worked as a luxury car salesman, I wouldn't have been exposed to the kind of people who reshaped my mindset.

Everything was connected. Every decision, every experience, it all lined up like stepping stones leading me to where I am today. And that's something you need to understand. Your network isn't just about business. It's about real, authentic relationships.

Forget trying to impress people just to get ahead. Instead, be the kind of person people want to be around. Be someone who adds value, who listens, who treats everyone with the same level of respect, no matter their status. Because when you move with kindness and authenticity, the right people naturally gravitate toward you. And the energy you put into the world? It comes back, often in ways you never expected.

And most importantly, never stay in one place. Growth doesn't happen in your comfort zone. Expose yourself to new environments, take risks, and meet new people. That one decision, that one introduction, that one moment of stepping outside your usual circle, could change everything.

Because being an underdog doesn't mean staying in the shadows. It means making bold moves, trusting your gut, and refusing to let circumstances dictate your path. Wakeboarding wasn't something people expected me to do because it was expensive, and out of reach for someone in my position. But I did it anyway. And that single decision? It led me to some of my biggest business opportunities, my strongest network, and a future I once thought was impossible.

So, take the leap. Build the relationships. Trust your instincts. Because the right connections, the right risks, and the right mindset can take you further than you ever imagined.

KEY TAKEAWAYS

The right mindset for networking is building authentic relationships. Networking isn't just about collecting business cards or growing your follower count; it's about fostering real, meaningful connections. Too often, people approach networking with a transactional mindset, thinking, "What can I get from this person?" Instead, the focus should be on "How can I add value to this person's life?"

Building authentic relationships means prioritizing trust, respect, and mutual benefit rather than short-term gains. People can sense insincerity from a mile away, and no one wants to feel like they're being used. When you genuinely care about others and seek to uplift them, you naturally attract valuable connections who will do the same for you.

Forget trying to impress people just to get ahead. Instead:

- **Be Valuable:** Relationships thrive on reciprocity, but too many people try to take before they give. If you want to build strong, lasting connections, focus on how you can contribute first. This doesn't mean offering grand gestures or financial favors. It can be as simple as sharing knowledge, making introductions, or offering support when needed. People appreciate those who bring value without expecting immediate returns. Over time, this generosity builds goodwill, and when you eventually need help or guidance, your network will be more than willing to support you in return.

- **Be Real:** People gravitate toward authenticity, not desperation. Whether in business or social circles, people can sense when someone is networking just for personal gain. Instead of trying too hard to be liked or to sell yourself, be yourself. Authenticity fosters trust, and trust is the foundation of strong relationships. Share your real thoughts, interests, and even vulnerabilities when appropriate. People connect more deeply when they see the human side of you rather than just a polished version.

- **Be Fearless:** Growth doesn't happen inside your comfort zone. Expanding your network means actively seeking out new experiences, environments, and people. Attend events, join communities, and engage in conversations that challenge you. If you always interact with the same people, you limit your opportunities for growth. Be open to meeting people from different industries, backgrounds, and perspectives. You never know what insights or opportunities they may bring. Even if social situations make you anxious, remember that confidence is built through repeated exposure. The more you put yourself out there, the easier it becomes.

- **Always Go the Extra Mile:** Do more of what you're tasked to do, always go beyond. The people who stand out in any field are those who consistently exceed expectations. Going the extra mile doesn't mean working yourself to exhaustion. It means taking pride in your work, delivering excellence, and adding unexpected value. Whether in business, networking, or friendships, being someone who consistently goes beyond what's required makes you memorable. When you do more than what is asked of you, people take notice and appreciate your efforts. This builds a strong reputation, which in turn strengthens your network.

- *KKK: Kapamilya, Kaibigan, at Kakilala* **(Family, Friends, and Acquaintances):** Your network starts with the people closest to you. Opportunities often come from unexpected connections, whether it's family, friends, or even casual acquaintances. Never underestimate the power of relationships—someone you barely know today could open doors for you tomorrow.

Networking is about cultivating real relationships based on trust, authenticity, and mutual value. The strongest networks are built by those who give before they take, stay genuine, step out of their comfort zones, and go the extra mile in every interaction. By focusing on the people around you, nurturing connections, and maintaining integrity, you create opportunities not just for yourself, but for others as well. When you approach networking with the right mindset, success follows naturally.

CHAPTER SEVEN

Building Trust And Integrity

"We are defined by the choices we make."

— Tyler Durden, Fight Club

I'll start this chapter with three stories of betrayal, each one from a close friend. These experiences taught me a valuable lesson about choosing the right people in both business and personal relationships. I hope as I share these with you, you take something valuable away from them.

The first betrayal came from a very close high school friend. We were close friends when we were young. Years later, he reached out and asked if I could refer him to a computer programmer for his business. I didn't pry, but I asked what kind of business it was so I could connect him with the right person. He vaguely mentioned it involved uploading videos but seemed hesitant to explain further. I let it go and referred him anyway. But it didn't stop there. He needed more people for his business and eventually, he was able to build up a team because of my referrals.

He told me he had made PHP 13 million in just 6 months. I was curious and asked what his business was, he just explained that it was online and that he only needed to upload videos. Then he turned to me and said, "You know, since you've been good to me, I'll treat you, let's go out of the country and celebrate!"

I realized that our friendship was something real and deep. To think that you'd treat your friend to an all-expense paid trip somewhere overseas, I mean who does that?

However, something changed after that. I was about to resign from the company I was working for, and my final pay and commission would have to be released a few months after I resigned. So, I thought of borrowing money from him and told him I would pay him back when I received my commission, to which he agreed.

So, I borrowed money from him, and the good thing was my last pay and commission arrived early, and I was able to pay him back before our agreed date.

Then to my surprise, he said, "I think I might need your help now. You see, I need a bit of money for the payroll of my team. Don't worry, I promise to pay it back, it's just that money's tight right now, and clients still have to pay a bit later than I expected."

I hesitated because I didn't have other means of income at that time. I'd just resigned, and the only money I had at that time was the last pay I'd received from the previous company. And I was also planning to save that money either for a business or for personal expenses.

Since he was my friend and I wanted to help him, I ended up letting him borrow my money.

He managed to pay back a small fraction of the borrowed amount after a month but abruptly disappeared after that. I discovered later from a friend who had also invested in his business that his business was involved in illegal activities. Consequently, his business started to fall when the credit card companies of his clients detected his fraudulent transactions and ceased paying him. This is why he borrowed the money from me so he could pay his team. Then, the rest is history.

Now, the second betrayal, and this was for me the heaviest, came after when I had my family. I talked about this a bit in the previous chapter, but I will talk more about it in detail.

It was the business I engaged in with two of my friends. Initially, it was a business that had been thriving for 13 years. They needed my expertise for the business, marketing-wise, rebranding, and so on.

All was set. I'd started doing the marketing, but I noticed that as time went by, I was seeing some misalignment in our values. First, they were not open to any of my suggestions for marketing, and second, they were not completely transparent with their vision for the business, which caused me to feel disconnected from the direction we were heading in.

In the end, I realized this business wasn't for me. Our partnership lacked balance, and I knew it wasn't going to work long-term.

So, I told them, "Hey you know what, we're friends but at the end of the day, for my own peace, I want out of the business. Whatever it is that I did with the business, I just want out. You can just bring back my money whenever you can."

But they didn't want to. They felt like I was leaving them because of the pandemic, which was not true. I felt like I wasn't respected and valued. Whenever I talked about how we could improve our marketing, I just heard harsh comments that were not even necessary. They would tell me that my vision was too high and too ambitious for them.

I also had a direction for the commercial side of the business that would take on a different storytelling narrative to pull the audience in. But for them, they didn't want to spend money on those investments in marketing. They preferred that I did it for free, but that wasn't possible because I had a team to pay.

So, from there, I'd already noticed that they didn't believe in my vision. I felt less respected, and valued, and there was no integrity in our partnership. If you ask me now, are we still friends? Well, I guess I would say yes, but I like to keep my distance from them as much as possible because I don't want to be disappointed again.

The third betrayal, and the most recent, was from a friend and my son's godmother. She wanted me to invest in a business that she was an agent for. It took her three years to persuade me, and the only reason I remember why I agreed was because she mentioned the name of my son and said that this was for him.

At the mere mention of my son, my heart softened. And to be honest, the interest was pretty high, so I said, "Okay, why not?" So, for the first 6 months, the business was doing well. I received my monthly investment on time.

Then after those 6 months, it began to crumble, and I wasn't receiving the remaining part of my investment. Now you may ask where the betrayal comes in, right? I mean it's not her fault that the business crashed, and it wasn't even her business to start with; she was just an agent.

Well, on my first investment, she asked me for a specific amount of money to invest in. Then, after 3 months, she asked for another amount of investment, and during this time, we already knew that the business was not doing well, based on rumors I'd heard from other investors. But still, she insisted on the second investment and assured me that even if the business failed, she would pay me in full. So, the betrayal comes from the fact that she already knew that the business was failing but she still insisted that I invest. Plus, her word when she said that she'd pay me in full even if things don't work out.

But she didn't. If you ask me if we're still friends? Yes, we are, and we're on good terms. Yes, there was a conflict, and I had a set of bad feelings toward her, but then I realized that at some point, I got caught up in the idea of making money fast and let greed get the best of me.

The common thing I noticed with these three betrayals was that all of them were really close friends of mine.

And you know what they say, third time's a charm. From here I'll tell you all the lessons I've learned so that you don't have to go through the same mistakes as I did when it comes to choosing a business partner or a partner in general (may it be a life partner, or a friend, etc.).

First, this experience taught me that if someone's values don't align with yours, don't force it. Not just in terms of choosing a business partner, but in general like when you do things that don't align with your true self, then don't push it further.

Looking back at all three of those betrayals, I already saw red flags. I already felt something was wrong even before pursuing it, but I was blinded by money. I was a dreamer, and I wanted a better life for me and my family. So even though I knew somehow that it was wrong because it didn't align with my values, I still risked it.

Second, don't always give your full trust. Only give about 70 to 80 percent of your trust, never all of it. Always leave something for yourself. Don't overshare, whether it's your ideas, your personal life, or your plans. You never know when someone might use it against you.

Third, never forget the red flags. They're there for a reason, but if you deliberately ignore them, like I did, trust me, you'll get in so much trouble and disappointment. So, save yourself that. And by red flags, I believe, we have our own red flags. For me, it's how you treat other people and the way you lead. You shouldn't be just the typical commanding person. You should also walk the talk.

I'm much smarter now about who I go into business with. However, my advice is that if you love someone, whether a friend or family member, think twice before making them your business partner. Your business partner should be someone you trust professionally. But don't get too comfortable, because at the end of the day, they're still their own person.

Not all of the stories I will mention here are bad. I'll share with you one story that also reflects building trust and integrity, and how this value eventually led to something good.

In a previous chapter, I shared with you my mental and financial struggles during the pandemic. But despite the circumstances, I still had the courage to refund all my clients' payments for the projects I'd booked with them for my production company. It wasn't stipulated in the contract; in fact, I mentioned that these were nonrefundable, but I still gave it back to them. I didn't think it was fair to them because most of us, if not all, suffered due to the pandemic.

I did lose some money, but I also gained new opportunities. After the pandemic, I closed multiple projects, which gave me the chance to establish a new business: a podcast that now has over 600k followers on social media.

So, you see, these three betrayals, although different in nature, all share the same core lesson: trust is fragile. Once broken, it's nearly impossible to restore.

And integrity? Well, when people lack integrity, they are capable of anything, deception, manipulation, betrayal. It's a harsh truth, but one that should be acknowledged.

Trust and integrity aren't just moral virtues; they are the key to long-term success in every aspect of life.

I'll never forget my first big sale as a luxury car salesman. Back then, I was hustling hard, learning the ropes, and trying to prove myself in an industry where reputation was everything. That's when I met my first client, a man who, at first glance, you'd never think was a billionaire.

This client of mine wasn't born rich. Far from it. Before becoming a business tycoon, he was a janitor, a waiter, and a blue-collar worker just trying to get by. He did whatever job to put food on the table. But as fate would have it, an Arab businessman saw something in him, believed in his potential, and helped him rise. Fast forward to today, he is now a known politician and a business tycoon. To make my point on how rich he is, this man can spend over PHP 150 million in a single night!

Years passed. I moved on from selling cars and built my career in marketing, video production, and digital business. I didn't think much about that first sale until recently, when our paths crossed again unexpectedly.

It was him.

But this time, he wasn't looking for a car. He and his running mate were looking for someone to direct their campaign materials, and a common friend referred me to them, without her knowing that I'd already met the business tycoon before. When I met with them, there was no hesitation in bringing me on board.

Why? Because trust doesn't expire. Credibility carries over, even when you switch industries. If you do right by people, they remember. And when the time comes, they will choose to work with you again.

This is why integrity in business is nonnegotiable. Some people think closing a sale is just about persuasion, but it's about building relationships that last beyond the transaction. When you gain someone's respect, you're not just making money, you're securing future opportunities, opening doors that you never even saw coming.

So, if there's one lesson to take from this, it's this: Treat every deal, every job, and every connection as if it's going to come back to you, because it will. Whether you're selling cars, producing videos, or running an empire, the way you handle people today will shape the opportunities you receive tomorrow.

In business, a solid reputation can open doors that skill alone cannot. In relationships, honesty fosters deep connections that withstand challenges. In leadership, integrity earns respect and loyalty from those who follow you. Without these things, you may achieve temporary success.

Being a dark horse means thriving in a world that often rewards deception and shortcuts. It means playing the long game, refusing to compromise your principles for temporary gain. It means understanding that real power doesn't come from manipulation or betrayal, it comes from being someone who people can trust, someone whose word carries weight.

So, as you move forward, ask yourself, are you someone people can trust? Do you hold yourself to a standard of integrity that sets you apart from the rest?

Because in the end, the only true power is the one that cannot be taken away—your reputation, your character, and the trust you've built over time.

KEY TAKEAWAYS/ACTION

Trust and integrity are the backbone of every relationship, whether in business, friendships, or personal growth. The way you handle trust, betrayal, and your personal values will define your reputation and long-term success. Here's how you can embody these principles in everyday life:

- **Trust Is Everything:** Trust takes years to build, seconds to break, and often, a lifetime to repair. The reality is, that once someone loses faith in you, even the strongest relationships may never fully recover. Trust is more than words; it's about consistent actions that prove reliability, honesty, and loyalty. Be mindful of how you handle trust. Never make promises you can't keep, and if you break trust, own up to it and take responsibility.

- **Integrity Is Your Foundation:** Success without integrity is temporary. There are countless examples of people who reached the top by cutting corners, lying, or manipulating others, only to lose it all when the truth caught up with them. Integrity means standing firm in your values, even when no one is watching. Live by a personal code of ethics. Before making any decision, ask yourself: "Would I be proud of this if the whole world knew?"

- **Betrayal Comes in Many Forms:** Not all betrayals are obvious. Some happen in subtle ways, such as disloyalty, deception, or people using you for personal gain. Whether in business, relationships, or mentorship, be selective about who you trust. Watch for patterns, not just words. Pay attention to actions, not just intentions. Trust people who show consistency, honesty, and loyalty over time.

- **Your Reputation Is Your Greatest Asset:** Guard your reputation fiercely and never compromises your values for short-term gain. Reputation takes years to build but only moments to destroy. In today's digital world, one wrong move can follow you forever. Never compromise your values for short-term gain, because your name and integrity will always be worth more than temporary success. Every decision you make either builds or destroys your reputation. Before acting, ask: "Will this decision align with my long-term vision?"

- **The Dark Horse Mindset Thrives on Integrity:** True power comes from being someone people can rely on, not someone who manipulates their way to the top. A dark horse doesn't rely on manipulation or shortcuts; they rise through resilience, work ethic, and being someone others can depend on. Be the person who follows through. If you say you'll do something, deliver every single time.

- **Your Purpose Is Greater than Your Pain:** Betrayal hurts, but it should never define you. Use it as fuel to push forward. Pain is temporary, but purpose is permanent. Every setback is an opportunity to grow stronger and push forward with even greater determination. Use setbacks as fuel. Instead of asking, "Why did this happen to me?" ask "What can I learn from this?"

- **Even if You Trust Someone Deeply, Always Leave Room for Yourself:** Blind trust can be dangerous. Even the people you love most can make mistakes or change over time. Protect your own interests while maintaining healthy relationships. Maintain independence. No matter how much you trust someone, never put yourself in a position where their betrayal could ruin you.

- **There's No Such Thing as Easy Money:** Scammers and manipulators promise quick wealth, but true success is built on hard work, discipline, and persistence. Anything that comes too easily often falls apart just as fast. Focus on long-term success. Commit to mastering your craft, outworking the competition, and staying patient.

- **Always Do Good, Because the Energy You Give Is the Energy You Receive:** What you put into the world always comes back to you. The way you treat people, the values you live by, and the choices you make shape your legacy. Choose wisely. Make a habit of doing the right thing, even when it's inconvenient. Your actions will define the kind of life you attract.

Trust, integrity, and resilience are the foundation of the Dark Horse Mindset. By living with unwavering principles, protecting your reputation, and staying true to your purpose, you set yourself up for lasting success, respect, and a legacy that outlives you.

PART THREE

INSPIRING CHANGE BY LIVING YOUR VALUES

CHAPTER EIGHT

Be An Expert On Something

FEAR has two meanings: Forget Everything and Run OR Face Everything and Rise. The Choice is yours." — **Zig Ziglar**

Letting fear control your emotions will only hold you back in life. But when you face your fears head-on and remain resilient, you open yourself up to greater opportunities. You have nothing to lose but more to gain.

So how have risk-taking and expertise shaped my life? For starters, many of the biggest decisions I've made weren't perfect. Some of them flopped completely. But the common thread? Almost all of them were born from taking a risk. Even when things didn't go as planned, I never let setbacks stop me, I kept pushing, kept learning, and kept trying.

Expertise is a game-changer. When people see you as an authority, opportunities start chasing you instead of the other way around. The more skilled you become, the easier it is to gain referrals and build a solid reputation.

But expertise doesn't happen overnight. I wasn't an expert when I started. Like anyone else, I started out as a beginner, but I took the risk to learn and improve my skills.

Looking back, I realize that every major success in my life started with a risk. And in this chapter, I'll walk you through how each of those risks led to the next, shaping the path that brought me here.

One of the biggest risks I faced early in my career came when I landed a job as a medical representative for a well-known infant formula company. Out of over 100 applicants, they narrowed it down to four, and in the end, I got the spot. The job came with a free car and a laptop, which was a great deal for someone who was just starting out. The salary wasn't that high, but since it was commission-based, I knew there was potential to earn more.

For 2 months, I studied medical terms and product details. My job was to sell infant formula to doctors, mainly pediatricians.

Then came the catch. I found out I was being assigned to a region in the far north of the country, about a 6 to 9-hour ride from where I lived. That meant uprooting myself, and most importantly, putting my relationship with my girlfriend (now my wife) to the test.

I had to decide.

On one hand, moving forward with the job could have opened doors to new opportunities in the medical field. But on the other hand, I knew the strain of long distance could cost me my relationship. And if I lost that, I would lose something far more valuable than a job.

So, I took the risk. The kind that most people don't talk about. I chose not to go.

Looking back, I can't imagine how different my life would have been if I had taken that assignment. Maybe I would have climbed the corporate ladder in the medical industry. But I also know that if I had gone, there's a good chance I wouldn't have ended up with my wife. And without her, I wouldn't be the man I am today.

People think that risk-taking is about saying yes. But sometimes, the biggest risk is knowing when to say no. It's about knowing which risks align with the life you want to build. In the end, risks aren't just about chasing bigger paychecks or career growth. Sometimes, the most valuable risks are the ones that protect what truly matters.

That wouldn't be the last time I had to make a tough decision. Years later, I found myself in the same position once more.

I was preparing to resign from my role as a sales director for a real estate company. Just as I was about to leave, my boss approached me with an offer. He asked if I was interested in joining a new project under another real estate company.

The catch? It was a startup, and the offer was significantly lower than what I was already earning.

At the same time, a major bank offered me a full-time marketing role. Good pay. Full security. No risks.

The startup, on the other hand, was risky. My contract was only for 6 months, meaning if I didn't perform well, they could let me go. But the upside? The commission structure was much higher. If I played my cards right and closed deals, I could earn twice as much, maybe even more!

Logically, most people would have chosen the bank. Without a doubt, it was the safer, more predictable, and more stable option.

I thought about it and realized that with the bank, I'd just be another employee. But with the startup, I'd be a pioneer. And in my heart and gut, I was leaning toward the real estate job more than the bank job.

That was what sealed my decision. I chose real estate.

Yes, the bank job was comfortable, but comfort never builds wealth. Taking the real estate job meant stepping into the unknown, but it also meant unlimited potential. High risk, high reward.

Sometimes, playing it safe is the riskiest move you can make. If I had taken the bank job, I might have had a steady paycheck, but I wouldn't have had the freedom to build something bigger. Choosing real estate put me in a position where my income was tied directly to my effort, skills, and determination, not just the number of hours I worked.

That's the thing about risk; it's about seeing beyond the comfort zone and betting on yourself. And when you're willing to take that leap of faith, the rewards can be greater than you ever imagined.

Taking risks also forced me to level up fast. When you put yourself in uncomfortable situations, ones where failure is not an option, you figure things out because you must. There's no backup plan. No safety net. You either make it work, or you don't.

This was the exact feeling when I was working with my first big client for a video shoot. We all have that defining moment when a major opportunity comes our way, one that can change everything. And when it does, you can't afford to let it slip by.

I knew I had the skills. I had done the work. But still, there was that little voice in my head: "What if I don't deliver? What if I mess this up? What if this is the end before I even get started?"

I had to shut that voice down.

And I got to be honest, I was still nervous during the shoot, but I had to bring my A-game, I had to set in my mind that this was going to work. I had to pep talk my people to do the same. For this to be successful, all of us had to deliver.

I won't lie, there were times early on when I took on projects that scared the hell out of me because I wasn't 100% sure I knew what I was doing. But I went all in anyway. And you know what? Every single time, I exceeded expectations.

That's why I have one rule: Always beat your last project. Overdeliver, but don't overpromise.

And if you're scared of taking risks? Do it anyway. Don't waste your life overthinking the what ifs. Fear keeps you trapped, and nothing ever grows in a comfort zone.

Let me tell you a quick story.

When I started wakeboarding, I knew a ton of wakeboarders who were insanely good at wakeboarding. Skill-wise, perhaps they were 9/10.

Then there was me.

I wasn't even close to their level. Maybe a 7/10 on a good day. But you know what? I wasn't afraid to put myself out there. I signed up for every competition I could. I put myself in situations where I had to adapt, improve, and perform under pressure.

And guess what? I didn't just get better.

I won.

You can be the most talented person in the room, but if you don't take risks, you'll always be stuck on the sidelines. Meanwhile, someone with half your talent but twice your courage will surpass you because they put themselves in the game.

Taking risks, especially when no one else believes in you, is what separates leaders from followers. People may doubt you at first, but when you start winning, they'll have no choice but to respect you.

The ones who win in life are the ones who take risks. Not the ones who play it safe.

What does all of this have to do with the Dark Horse Mindset, you might ask?

Everything.

If you want to be an expert, you must be willing to take risks. Expertise isn't built in safe, comfortable environments, it's built in high-stakes situations where you're forced to figure things out under pressure. The more you put yourself in these situations, the faster you develop the skills, confidence, and experience needed to excel.

Beyond that, risk earns your respect. People don't admire those who hesitate; they respect those who act. When you bet on yourself and succeed, you prove to others, and more importantly to yourself, that you belong at the top. Even if you fail, you gain something valuable: experience, knowledge, and resilience.

Risk separates the dark horses from everyone else. The Dark Horse Mindset is about playing by your own rules, rising despite the odds, and taking bold, calculated risks that others are too scared to take. The ones who refuse to take risks stay exactly where they are, stuck in the same cycle, watching from the sidelines. But those who step up, put themselves out there, and push past fear? They're the ones who win. Because at the end of the day, it's not just about being good at something; it's about having the guts to show the world that you can.

Fear never disappears. But the ones who succeed are the ones who move forward anyway. Take the risk. Bet on yourself. And prove them wrong.

KEY TAKEAWAYS

- **Pursue Obsession, Gain Success (POGS):** Success doesn't come from half-hearted efforts, it comes from obsession. The people who make it to the top aren't just passionate; they're consumed by what they do. They wake up thinking about it, spend every waking hour perfecting their craft, and go to sleep strategizing how to be better. That level of focus and dedication naturally separates them from the rest. If you want to win, don't just "like" what you do—live and breathe it. Let your obsession fuel your progress, and success will follow.

- **Achieve Something First to Earn Respect. Walk the Talk:** No one takes advice from someone who hasn't done the work themselves. If you want to be respected, don't just talk about what you're going to do; prove it through action.

- **High Risk, High Reward:** Playing it safe might keep you comfortable, but it will never make you great. Every major success story has one thing in common. Risk. Whether it's leaving a stable job, investing in yourself, or taking on a challenge, you don't feel 100% ready for—risk is what creates opportunities. Sure, failure is always a possibility, but so is extraordinary success. And if you do fail? You don't lose, you learn. The greater the risk, the greater the potential for reward. If you never bet on yourself, you'll never know what you're truly capable of.

- **Specialization Beats Generalization:** Being decent at many things won't make you an expert. Find your niche, go deep, and become the go-to person in that area.

- **Reinvention Is Part of Growth:** Expertise isn't static. Stay ahead of the curve by evolving, adapting, and reinventing yourself when necessary. Those who remain flexible and open to change always stay relevant.

By embracing risk, obsession, and continuous learning, you'll not only become an expert but also open doors to opportunities you never imagined possible.

CHAPTER NINE

Giving Value

"Remember that the happiest people are not those getting more, but those giving more." — **H. Jackson Brown Jr.**

There is great power in giving, without expecting it to be returned. Give freely. Give because you can. The impact will come back in ways you never expected.

That's how the universe works. Energy is like a boomerang; it always returns in some ways. But before you can truly give value to others, you must start with yourself.

Before you can give value to others, you must value yourself first. When you genuinely value yourself, your actions will naturally follow and create value for others. Not because you're trying to prove something, but because you have so much to give.

This is the idea behind our podcast, "Life Over Whiskey."

The podcast didn't come from a business plan. Instead, it came from a love for meaningful and authentic conversations shared by real people. I used to spend hours talking about life, growth, and experiences with one of my close friends over whiskey. So, I thought, what if we made this into something bigger? What if these conversations and stories could help others, too?

"Life Over Whiskey" was inspired by two podcasts. A local one that was heartwarming and inspiring, with real stories that touched the soul, and an international podcast that delivered raw, unfiltered, and direct content.

I wanted "Life Over Whiskey" to be a mix of both, heartwarming yet deep, authentic, and real.

But this idea was just an idea at first. I didn't really know how to start a podcast. But eventually, the universe heard my thoughts and referred someone my way.

I talked about this in the previous chapter. But what I didn't tell you is that the podcast started with a fateful call to my technical director (now my co-host), "Hey bro, do you want to start a podcast called Life Over Whiskey?"

Our mission was clear, to create something that people could take value from, beyond just entertainment or virality. We wanted to share real lessons, real experiences, and real struggles that others could relate to. And at the same time, it was a way for us to showcase our work.

During the COVID-19 pandemic, the podcast became a platform for our businesses, my ad agency, AYO Creatives, and my production company, Paper St. Production, and his event agency, Cloud Studio.

Unexpectedly, "Life Over Whiskey" became something bigger than just a marketing tool. It became a safe space where we could genuinely help people through our conversations. It became a business, attracting sponsors, collaborations, and even opportunities we never imagined.

To give a voice to those who don't have a platform is something I had always wanted to do. When you genuinely give out of sincerity, opportunities will eventually come. Not because you chased them, but because you created something meaningful and impactful, touching the lives of others.

It's not always immediate, but it leaves an imprint. Sometimes, a single conversation can change the way someone sees their struggles. It can remind them they're not alone. That they can keep going. And that alone is enough.

That's how the universe works. Energy is like a boomerang; it always comes back to you in some way. But before you can truly give value to others, you must start with yourself.

That's exactly what happened next.

I had just bought a truck, originally intended for mobile music production, basically for music producers to rent, but

I saw something bigger. Instead of limiting it to just music, I wanted to turn it into a space where voices could be heard, literally.

So, I partnered with my co-host, and a content creator we had previously guested, saw its potential, and joined in. I called it "Kreative Truck" at first, then eventually called it "Pod Truck." It was the first roving podcast studio truck in the Philippines.

The Pod Truck became more than just a business. It became a movement, an opportunity for those with messages worth sharing to finally have a space to amplify their voices. And that's what continues to drive us today. Creating something bigger than ourselves, something that empowers others to speak, connect, and inspire.

Giving value isn't just about business, money, or success. It's about creating something that lasts. Something that outlives you. For me, this is about legacy. I want to leave behind something meaningful, not just for myself, but for my family. Because when you do good for others, that goodness has a way of coming back. Maybe not today, maybe not tomorrow, but someday. And even when I'm no longer here, I know my children and wife will be surrounded by the energy I put out into the world. Because that's how life works.

The more you focus on helping others, the more opportunities come back to you. And in my career, that mindset changed everything.

For three years straight, I was the leading sales director in the real estate company I was working for, not because I had the most aggressive sales tactics, but because I focused on giving more instead of thinking how it would benefit me. While everyone else was chasing quotas, I was building relationships. I wasn't just closing sales, I listened to what my clients needed, even if it didn't benefit me directly. My goal was simple: make their lives easier, solve their problems, and give them real value.

And because of that, the numbers took care of themselves. My clients trusted me. And when people trust you, they stick with you. That consistency, that commitment to always delivering more than expected, led to my biggest win yet: my promotion to senior sales director.

I didn't get there by chasing titles or commissions. I got there by playing the long game. And most people think this is hard to do. Well, it is. This kind of thinking isn't just a habit, it's a mindset. But before I could give value to others, I had to give value to myself first. It's like they say, you can't pour from an empty cup.

This is where self-introspection comes in. And the tool that helped me in my journey is hypnotherapy. It played a huge role in helping me heal and reconnect with myself.

I remember the first time I tried hypnotherapy. I was skeptical as hell. I thought, there's no way this is gonna work on me. But during the pandemic, I was so depressed. My mind felt like a battlefield, and I needed something, anything, to quiet the noise.

I walked into that session with my guard up, but what happened next shocked me to my core. It wasn't some magic trick or mind control. But hypnotherapy was this deep, honest conversation with me. During these sessions, the hypnotherapist would ask you a set of questions that were designed to guide you back to the parts of yourself you had buried under years of doubt, fear, and conditioning.

For the first time, I stopped running from my thoughts. I sat with them and let them surface. I rewrote the ones holding me back and discovered parts of myself I never knew existed.

Hypnotherapy helped me understand the why behind my struggles, why I had certain fears, and why I kept sabotaging myself. Because once you know the why, you have to decide what you are going to do with it.

You can use that knowledge to stay stuck, or you can use it to rewrite your story.

It was about accepting myself, even the messy, imperfect parts. That's what made me better at helping others. When you hear from a place of love instead of shame, you don't just survive, you thrive, and you become stronger, and more indispensable.

At its core, the Dark Horse Mindset is about becoming invaluable. It's about focusing on what you can give rather than what you can take. The world rewards those who create impact, who solve real problems, and who bring something valuable to the table. That's why the people who win in the long run aren't the ones constantly looking for shortcuts or validation. They're the ones who build something bigger than themselves.

And that all starts with you.

You can't pour into others if you're running on empty. You can't build value in the world if you don't first recognize your own worth.

The work begins from within rewriting the limiting beliefs, breaking free from the mental chains holding you back, and becoming the kind of person who naturally attracts opportunities.

Because when you operate from a place of self-worth and abundance, giving value isn't a strategy. It's just who you are. Like it becomes a part of you.

That's what separates the dark horses from the rest. While others are busy chasing, they're creating. While others focus on getting, they focus on giving.

And in the end, they don't just succeed.

They leave a legacy.

KEY TAKEAWAYS

- **Start with Self-Love:** You can't pour from an empty cup. The more you value yourself, the more you can give to others. Before you can genuinely provide value to the world, you have to believe in your own worth. True giving starts with a full heart. When you invest in your growth, heal your wounds, and recognize your own potential, you naturally have more to offer.

- **Give without Expecting Anything in Return:** True value isn't transactional. The universe will always reciprocate in ways you don't expect. Too many people give with strings attached, expecting immediate returns, recognition, or favors in exchange. But when you genuinely help others, opportunities will come, but not always in the way you expect. It might not be today, tomorrow, or even next year. But the energy you put out always finds its way back. Success is a byproduct of value, not the other way around.

- **Share Your Story:** You never know who might need to hear it. Your experiences, struggles, and lessons could be exactly what someone else needs. Whether through a podcast, a social media post, or a simple conversation, sharing your story creates a connection. And connection is what creates real impact.

- **Be Intentional with Your Impact:** Whether it's through conversations, your work, or simple acts of kindness, focus on leaving something meaningful behind. Every action has an effect, whether we realize it or not. Some people coast through life unaware of the influence they have on others, while dark horses understand that everything, they do have the potential to create a ripple effect.

- **Legacy Isn't about Money:** Many people chase wealth, thinking it will secure their legacy. But the reality is that money fades, titles disappear, and status is temporary. What people will remember is how you made them feel, how you helped them grow, and how you changed their lives. Your legacy is built in the moments when you uplift, empower, and create something bigger than yourself. It's about how you make people feel and the value you bring to their lives. That is what truly lasts.

- **Small Acts of Kindness Create a Massive Impact:** People often think they need to make a grand gesture to provide value, but sometimes, the smallest things leave the biggest mark. A kind word, a genuine compliment, or simply being present when someone needs you can be life changing. You never know what battle someone is fighting, and a single act of kindness can change their trajectory. The world doesn't need more takers. It needs more people willing to uplift others in small but meaningful ways.

- **Teach What You Know Because Knowledge Is Power:** If you've learned something that made your life better, share it. The fastest way to grow is to help others grow with you. Whether it's mentoring, coaching, or simply passing down wisdom, the more you give, the more you evolve.

- **Giving Value Makes You Unforgettable and Indispensable:** In a world where most people are focused on "What's in it for me?", being someone who consistently provides value sets you apart. People remember those who helped them, guided them, or gave them an opportunity when no one else did. If you want to leave a lasting impact, focus on how you can make other people's lives better because that's the real key to influence and legacy.

CHAPTER TEN

Negotiation And Persuasion

"Life is a negotiation." — **George J Sidle**

Every day is a negotiation. The choices we make, whether big or small, shape our future more than we realize.

Do I go to work today? Do I go to the gym? What do I eat? These little decisions shape our lives more than we realize. The ability to make strong, confident choices is what separates great negotiators from the rest.

Your decision-making skills determine your success, and success is something you earn. It comes from hard work, failures, and experiences that refine your wisdom and resilience.

But you know, everyone makes bad decisions at some point, and that's normal. What matters is learning from them. As you gain experience, you start recognizing patterns, refining your instincts, and making wiser choices. Every failed negotiation or sour deal is just another stepping stone toward mastering the game of life.

Take something as simple as deciding to hit the gym. Some days, I don't feel like going. But I know that if I choose to go, I'm essentially negotiating for a longer, healthier life. And if I push myself beyond my usual one-hour routine and stay for two? The results compound. I become stronger, healthier, and more confident, and that mindset bleeds into all areas of my life.

The same goes for work–life balance. Every day, I negotiate between grinding at work and spending time with my family. If I work too much, I sacrifice personal moments and my health. If I spend too much time at home, I risk slowing down my career. The key is finding the right balance, something I consciously juggle daily.

But some negotiations have life-changing results.

There are moments in life that change everything. One of mine happened on November 1. If you can recall, I discussed this in the previous chapter where it was a holiday and everyone took a day off, but I made a different choice. I volunteered to work. Then that decision led me to one of my biggest clients and closed one of the biggest sales of my life.

And that one sale became the foundation of my entire career. It gave me the funds to start my production company. It positioned me as a key player in the industry. It opened doors I never imagined possible, eventually leading to my director role in a high-end real estate company.

I could have taken the holiday like everyone else. But I negotiated with myself: "Do I take a break, or do I seize an opportunity?" I took the chance, and it paid off beyond what I could have predicted.

Sometimes, the most pivotal negotiations are the ones you have with yourself. Success belongs to those who go the extra mile when others won't. Negotiation isn't just about money or deals. It's about relationships. One of the best ways to win in any relationship, business or personal, is to always give more than expected.

But my journey in real estate wasn't always like this. In fact, my very first sale almost didn't happen.

It happened when I was about to give up.

Remember the story in the Introduction? She was my first sale, my breakthrough.

Sometimes, everything you've worked for, everything you've struggled through, boils down to a single moment. A moment where you stand at a crossroads, on the brink of giving up or taking one last shot.

I didn't know it then, but I was standing at that very moment.

Months of trying, failing, and getting nowhere had drained me. That night, I was ready to pack it in. I started putting my stuff away, already thinking about what's next. Thinking that this wasn't for me. That it was time to cut my losses and move on.

Then, I saw her. And something in my gut told me to go for it. One last try.

And you know, until now, I still couldn't believe it when she told me "yes." I almost couldn't believe it. After months of rejection, I finally had someone interested.

She bought two units from me, then eventually an entire floor.

I was in shock. After months of nothing, I had finally made my first sale.

That one moment, where I could have packed up and gone home, but instead took one more shot, changed my life.

Persuasion isn't just about closing a sale; it's also about being real and authentic. People smell desperation and they don't buy from scripts.

Because you never know when that one conversation will change everything.

But closing that sale was just the beginning. I made sure to stay connected with the client who trusted me, even after the deal was done. We became friends and, over time, that client kept returning to buy more properties from me.

And even better! She started referring international clients to me, turning into a repeat and referral powerhouse. In return, I made sure to reward her referrals with incentives.

That one negotiation changed everything. And it all started with the decision to push forward when I could have given up.

The best deals aren't about money. They're about relationships that last. Sometimes, that means going above and beyond, like personally helping a client buy furniture because they didn't have time or remembering them on their birthdays.

Small things, but they make a huge impact on those people you're helping.

And it's not just clients; I apply the same principle to my team.

Unlike bosses who just command from the top, I invest in my people. I take time to know them personally. I treat them to team building activities and reward them with incentives out of my own pocket. I even stay up late to listen when they call and need someone to talk to. Come to think of it, that's not part of my job anymore, but I do it because I genuinely care.

I had a team member who was struggling with sales because he was naturally introverted. Through our conversations, I helped him identify what truly motivated him. He realized his biggest goal was to reunite with his family abroad. That clarity gave him the drive to step out of his comfort zone, and to keep on pushing forward.

When you empower others, it creates a ripple effect. Kindness and generosity always come back in ways you never expect. Not to brag, but my team genuinely loves coming to work—not just because of the success we achieve, but because we've built a workplace that inspires them to grow, feel safe, and do their best.

But beware, people can sense when you're genuine or fake. If you don't actually care, people will feel it. That's why I always try to find something in common with every person I meet. Not as a sales tactic, but because I value human connection.

So, I ask you, how do you want to be treated? If you expect respect, kindness, and generosity from others, you must embody those traits first.

That's why I make sure that every deal, every relationship, every negotiation is built on trust. It's why I never cut corners. When people see that you deliver value beyond what's expected, they remember you, and they keep coming back.

Good energy attracts good results. The way you treat people today shapes your future success. Never underestimate the power of kindness in negotiation.

Negotiation and persuasion aren't just business skills, they're life skills. The foundation of success in every aspect of life. Every choice, every decision you make is a negotiation with yourself. Every conversation is an opportunity to influence, open doors, and shape your future. Master these skills, and you don't just survive; you dominate.

The most powerful negotiators aren't the ones who only focus on their own gain. They're the ones who create win-win situations. They're the ones who build relationships, establish trust, and go the extra mile.

That's what separates a dark horse from the rest. While others negotiate for short-term gains, a dark horse plays the long game. They understand that success is built on more than just deals, it's built on trust, reputation, and genuine connections.

So next time you're faced with a decision, ask yourself:

Are you negotiating for the short term or the long term?

Are you giving just enough, or are you going the extra mile?

Are you just selling, or are you building relationships?

It's about building an unshakable reputation, earning respect, and forging alliances that stand the test of time.

Because in the end, the energy you put out is the energy you receive. If you want success, negotiate wisely, persuade with integrity, and always go the extra mile.

KEY TAKEAWAYS

- **Grit and Resiliency**: Success usually comes right after you feel like giving up. Push through. The toughest moments are often the gateway to the biggest breakthroughs. Train yourself to see failure as feedback and use it to come back stronger.

- **Always Have a Purpose and Goal**: Clarity fuels negotiation. Know your purpose, then go after it. Without a clear goal, you're just reacting to circumstances instead of shaping them. Whether it's a business deal or a personal decision, always ask yourself: What do I want to achieve, and how do I get there?

- **Believe You Are Destined for a Good Life**: Your mindset shapes your reality. If you negotiate from a place of desperation, you'll settle for less. But when you believe in your own worth and potential, you naturally attract better opportunities and make smarter decisions. Never forget that you set the tone for your own success.

- **Go the Extra Mile:** People remember those who give more than they take. Whether it's adding extra value in business or simply being a reliable friend, going the extra mile creates lasting connections and future opportunities.

- **Negotiate for the Long Game**: Short wins are nice, but lasting relationships are the real game-changer. Every deal, every conversation, every opportunity should be seen through the lens of the future. Will this decision help you build something bigger? Will it reinforce trust and reputation? Play for legacy, not just quick rewards.

- **Build Relationships, Not Transactions:** Persuasion and negotiation aren't about slick words or manipulation. They're about forming genuine human connections. The strongest deals happen when people trust you, not because you have the best pitch, but because they believe in you. Focus on relationships first, and business will follow.

- **Master the Art of Self-Negotiation:** The toughest negotiations are the ones you have with yourself. Every day, you decide whether to push forward or make excuses. Discipline is the foundation of success. If you can master your own mind, your external negotiations will become second nature.

- **Be Willing to Walk Away:** Not every opportunity is worth taking. Desperation leads to bad deals. Confidence, on the other hand, comes from knowing your worth. If a situation doesn't align with your values or goals, have the courage to walk away. The right opportunity will come, and you'll be ready when it does.

- **Actions Speak Louder Than Words:** You can say all the right things, but if your actions don't back them up, people won't trust you. The best negotiators don't rely on talk alone—they prove their value through consistency, reliability, and results. Show up, follow through, and let your actions persuade you.

- **Energy Is Everything:** People don't just respond to what you say, they respond to how you make them feel. If you bring positivity, confidence, and generosity into a negotiation, it will be felt. Approach every deal, conversation, and relationship with the mindset of creating value, and you'll always come out ahead.

- **Adapt and Evolve:** The best negotiators are those who are able to adapt and evolve quickly. Every situation, every deal, and every relationship require a different approach. Stubbornness kills opportunity, but flexibility opens doors. Be willing to pivot, learn, and adjust your strategy to fit the moment. Growth comes from those who embrace change, not those who resist it.

CHAPTER ELEVEN

Accept And Move Forward

"My mama always said life was like a box of chocolates. You never know what you're gonna get" — **Forrest Gump**

My son has Down syndrome.

We found out when my wife was 21 weeks pregnant. It was supposed to be just a routine scan, a check-up to make sure everything was fine. I was always there for her appointments, but this was the one time I wasn't.

The doctor saw markers, chromosomal signs that pointed to Down syndrome. Her pregnancy was suddenly classified as high-risk. Every two weeks, she had to go for ultrasounds, and each time, the markers became more obvious.

The reality was sinking in for her.

I wasn't scared. Not at first. The doctor told us there was still a chance that everything could be normal. And honestly, we never thought we'd have a child with special needs. There was no history of it in our family, and like most people, we assumed that was how it worked. But the truth? It's not about genetics, but it was a game of chance. A random mutation in the 21st chromosome; 1 in 800 babies are born with Down syndrome every day.

I reassured my partner. I told her no matter what, we'd go through this together. But as the pregnancy went on, and the markers increased, I could see how much it worried her. The doctors told us not to panic. They'd seen cases where the markers were there, but the baby was born without any condition.

When my son was born, I knew immediately. The moment I saw his eyes, I just knew.

I can't explain the feeling. It was a mix of emotions, happiness, sadness, and confusion. It wasn't what I expected. As a dad, you have expectations, you imagine your son looking like you, maybe even better. You start to build this picture in your head, and you see them growing up, playing sports with you, and bonding over your hobbies. But reality gives you something else.

It was already overwhelming to be a first-time parent. But a first-time parent for a kid with special needs? It was nerve-wracking. Add the doctors and specialists constantly checking on your baby, blood tests, x-rays, you name it, they were constantly in and out of the room.

I started questioning God. Why this? Why me? Out of all the millions of people out there, why was I the one chosen for this? Especially when I was already carrying so much on my shoulders.

It was hard to accept and swallow the fact that my son would be in this condition for the rest of his life. But more than anything, I was scared of the future. What happens when me and my wife are gone? Who's going to take care of him? Will he be okay in this world?

We had no answers. But we knew we couldn't stay in that space forever. We had to move forward, even if we didn't know how yet.

That's when our doctor introduced us to the Down Syndrome Association of the Philippines (DSAPI). They became our lifeline. They reassured us that we weren't alone, that other families had walked this path before us.

They told us something I would only fully understand later: "One day, you'll see why your son was given to you."

And I realized they were right. God doesn't make mistakes. He gave us my son for a reason. And I looked at him and saw everything I wish I could be pure, loving, kind, and patient. He loved without hesitation. He found joy in the simplest things.

If my son had been born into a family that didn't have the patience, the love, or the resources to raise a child with special needs, what would have happened to him?

Life will throw things at you that you never saw coming. It will shatter your expectations and force you onto a path you never planned for. And when that happens, you have two choices. You fight it and get stuck in the "what should have been." Or you accept it, adapt, and you find beauty in the path you were given.

This is the Dark Horse Mindset.

You might not land where you planned, but that doesn't mean you aren't exactly where you're supposed to be.

There's a poem called Welcome to Holland by Emily Perl Kingsley that explains it perfectly. It's about someone planning a trip to Italy, but their plane lands in Holland instead. Just imagine, you've planned everything you're going to visit in Italy, the places you'll visit, the foods you'll try, but then along the way something unexpected happens and you're forced to land in Holland instead. So, you must go out and buy new guidebooks. And you must learn a whole new language, and you will meet a whole new group of people you would never have met. It's just a different place, it's slower paced than Italy, less flashy than Italy, but after you've been there a while and you catch your breath, you look around and you begin to notice that Holland has windmills and tulips and all those beautiful things Italy doesn't have.

And that's life.

You can spend forever mourning the fact that you didn't land in Italy. Or you can open your eyes, take a deep breath, and realize Holland is beautiful too.

Most people get stuck in regret, frustration, and resistance. They hold onto the dream that didn't happen, instead of seeing the opportunity in front of them.

But if you want to win in life, you have to accept, adapt, and move forward.

Whether it's in business, relationships, or personal challenges, you're going to face things you never planned for. And if you fight against reality, you'll lose. Every. Single. Time.

But if you embrace what is, instead of what should have been? You'll find strength, clarity, and purpose.

Now while we were dealing with everything with my son, something else came up.

Before my mom passed away, she and her sister had inherited the ancestral house of my grandparents. But she didn't leave my share of the house directly to me, she left it to her sister, my aunt. My mom did this to protect me from myself. I was young, reckless, and she knew I could spend all the money. She left the deed of donation to my aunt. So the plan was simple: when I was old enough, my share would come back to me.

But my aunt also told me not to rely too much on this inheritance, knowing full well that their other siblings (their brothers) also wanted a share of it. To put it in context, their other brothers had already received their share of the inheritance in the form of stocks and cash, so the house was given to my aunt and my mom.

Fast forward to 10 years later. I was successful and was able to buy my own assets, including a condominium. Then my aunt came home from abroad and we had the opportunity to talk about the inheritance. She said she will take care of it and eventually told me that what was mine, would be mine. She even told me to sell the house, take my share in cash, and use her share to buy a condominium next to mine.

But when my aunt passed, things didn't go according to plan.

My uncles took over everything, including my share of the inheritance. And the worst part? I had to buy back what was already mine because I had no choice.

At that time, my wife had just given birth to my son, and knowing his condition, there were a lot of expenses since there were numerous tests he had to take. Plus, I had just purchased the condo, so my money was really tight. I had no savings. So, I had to apply for a bank loan to pay my share to my mom's brothers, and to transfer the deed of the house to my name. Because of this, even my relationships with my cousins have been affected.

But resentment doesn't change the past. It just chains you to it, to all that negative energy. And like I've said before, I truly believe that the energy you put out is the energy you get back.

So, I let go. I stopped being bitter about what was taken and started focusing on what I could build. Because at the end of the day, your future isn't about what you inherit—it's about what you create. I didn't dwell on the problem, I dwelled on the solution. I knew I had to take action immediately.

This was my wake-up call. If I wanted my kids to have something, I had to build it myself. Wealth. Security. A legacy. Not just money, but values so they'd never feel entitled to a handout, and they'd never be in a position where someone could take what was theirs.

That's what dark horses do. They don't waste time wishing things were different. They take what is and make the best of it, and that applies to everything in life. You get up. You grind. You build. And when life knocks you down, you move forward stronger. Because at the end of the day, the only thing life truly owes you is what you earn.

KEY TAKEAWAYS

- **Acceptance Over Resistance**: Life is unpredictable. No matter how well you plan, there will always be moments when things don't go as expected. It's easy to resist change, to cling to what was or dwell on what could have been, but this only keeps you stuck in frustration and disappointment. Resistance creates suffering, while acceptance creates clarity. Acceptance doesn't mean giving up or passively accepting failure. It means acknowledging reality for what it is and choosing to adapt rather than waste energy fighting what you can't change. When you accept the situation, you free yourself to explore new solutions, uncover hidden opportunities, and move forward with purpose. The strongest people aren't the ones who never face setbacks; they're the ones who embrace life's unpredictability and turn obstacles into stepping stones.

- **Let Go and Move On**: Holding onto resentment, regret, or past failures is like carrying a heavy backpack up a mountain; it only slows you down. It's natural to feel anger, disappointment, or sadness when things don't go your way, but staying trapped in those emotions prevents you from making progress. Letting go doesn't mean forgetting or pretending something didn't hurt. It means making peace with the past and refusing to let it dictate your future. The more you dwell on what went wrong, the less energy you have to create something better. Instead of replaying past mistakes or wishing things had been different, ask yourself: What can I learn from this? How can I use this experience to grow? Moving on is an act of self-liberation. When you release negativity, you create space for new opportunities, relationships, and successes to enter your life.

- **Strength Comes from Adaptability**: Many people mistake strength for control. They believe that if they can just manage every detail of their lives, they can prevent failure, disappointment, or pain. But the reality is, no one has absolute control over everything. True strength comes not from controlling every outcome but from being adaptable in the face of uncertainty. Adaptability is what allows you to turn unexpected changes into new possibilities. When one path is blocked, a strong person doesn't stand there, frustrated and defeated; they find another way. This mindset is what separates those who succeed from those who stay stuck. Think of nature: the strongest trees don't resist the wind; they bend with it. In the same way, the strongest individuals don't rigidly fight against change; they adjust, recalibrate, and find ways to thrive no matter the circumstances.

- **Seek Support When Needed**: Society often glorifies the idea of self-reliance, making it seem like asking for help is a sign of weakness. But in reality, the most successful people understand that no one achieves greatness alone. Whether it's mentors, friends, family, or a community that shares your struggles, having the right people in your corner can make all the difference. Seeking support doesn't mean offloading your problems onto others; it means recognizing that we're stronger together. The right advice, encouragement, or even just knowing that someone understands what you're going through can be the push you need to keep going. Surround yourself with people who uplift and challenge you, and don't be afraid to lean on them when necessary. No one succeeds in isolation. Find your tribe, build strong relationships, and be willing to both give and receive support when needed.

- **Your Legacy Is What You Build:** Success isn't measured by what you were born into, what you lost, or what advantages others had; it's defined by what you create with the resources, skills, and mindset you develop. Many people spend their lives comparing themselves to others, feeling like they started at a disadvantage or that they don't have the same opportunities. But your true legacy isn't based on external factors; it's built by your actions, resilience, and the impact you leave behind. Think of the people who inspire you the most. Chances are, they didn't have an easy path. They faced setbacks, failures, and uncertainty, yet they created something meaningful despite the odds. Your journey is no different. Every choice you make, every lesson you learn, and every challenge you overcome shape your legacy. Instead of focusing on what you don't have, focus on what you can build with what you do have. Success is about innovation, persistence, and the willingness to create something new when circumstances change.

- **The Dark Horse Mindset:** A dark horse is someone who defies expectations, someone who rises despite challenges, setbacks, or being underestimated. This mindset is about resilience, the ability to get up every time life knocks you down. It's about seeing every setback as an opportunity for a comeback. Dark horses don't dwell on failures. They don't make excuses. They don't wait for the perfect opportunity; they create it. They trust in their ability to adapt, learn, and push forward, no matter how difficult the road ahead looks. The difference between those who succeed and those who don't isn't talent, luck, or privilege but the ability to keep going when things get tough. No matter what happens, remember: you are not defined by your circumstances, but by how you respond to them. When life gets difficult, when plans fall apart, when challenges feel overwhelming, embrace the Dark Horse Mindset. Rise, adapt, and move forward. Strength isn't about avoiding the struggle; it's about pushing through it and coming out stronger on the other side.

Life will always throw unexpected challenges your way. You can choose to resist them and stay stuck, or you can accept, adapt, and use them as stepping stones to something greater. Let go of the past, be adaptable, seek support when needed, and focus on what you can build rather than what you've lost. Your strength isn't in controlling everything, it's in making the best of every situation. And when you adopt the

Dark Horse Mindset, nothing can keep you down for long. Keep moving forward, and success will follow.

PARTING THOUGHTS

Before you close this book, I want you to take a breath and look back on your journey: your struggles, your wins, and the moments that nearly broke you.

Think back to the moments when you felt stuck, defeated, or on the verge of giving up. When you were knocked down so hard, getting up seemed pointless.

Maybe you're in that place right now. If you are, I want you to remember this: Every setback, every rejection, and every failure is simply a stepping stone leading you to your breakthrough.

I don't just believe this. I know it because I've lived it.

I'll never forget that night when I stood along the busy city streets, handing out flyers. Exhausted and questioning my worth. I had no idea that just 24 hours later, my entire reality would shift. If I had walked away just one moment sooner, if I had given in to the doubt creeping into my mind, I would have never met the person who paved the way for my real estate career path.

But that wasn't the only time life tested me. During the pandemic, everything I had worked so hard for was on the brink of collapse. Clients disappeared overnight. Money stopped coming in. I watched my savings dwindle, unsure of what would happen next. I felt the crushing weight of uncertainty, and for a brief moment, I thought maybe this was it. Maybe I've lost it all.

But I refused to accept that. Because if there's one thing I've learned, it's this: the Dark Horse doesn't crumble under pressure it adapts, it fights, and it rises. So, I pivoted. Eventually, I didn't just recover, I came back stronger than ever. That moment of near collapse became the foundation for an even greater success.

Life is unpredictable. It will test you, break you, and push you to your limits. But in those moments, you have a choice: stay down or rise up.

The Dark Horse Mindset is about defying the odds. It's about realizing that success is not reserved for the lucky or the privileged. It's for those who refuse to quit. It's for those who push past their breaking points, defy expectations, and create opportunities where others see dead ends.

Every chapter in this book has been a piece of that mindset, each one a step toward becoming the person who refuses to be overlooked, underestimated, or left behind. Let's bring it all together.

In Chapter 1, we discussed Self-Awareness and Having a Goal and Purpose. The foundation of the Dark Horse

Mindset is knowing who you are and where you're going. Without self-awareness, you'll be running in circles, chasing goals that don't truly align with you. Success starts with a clear vision of knowing your strengths, weaknesses, and the unique value you bring to the world.

In Chapter 2, we talked about Enhancing Your Physical Appearance and Knowing How to Present Yourself. Your presence speaks before you even open your mouth. How you present yourself to the world, your posture, style, and confidence, affects how people perceive you. The way you carry yourself can open doors or close them before you even step inside.

In Chapter 3, we explored Mental Fortitude and Turning Your Pain into Power. Pain is inevitable, but suffering is optional. The Dark Horse Mindset embraces hardship as fuel for growth. Every setback is an opportunity to rise stronger. The strongest people aren't the ones who have never struggled, they're the ones who have faced the storm and walked through it.

In Chapter 4, we covered Humility and Learning How to Deal with All Walks of Life. You can learn something from everyone, and no one is too small to teach you a lesson. The Dark Horse Mindset requires you to stay grounded, listen more than you speak, and treat everyone with respect because you never know who holds the key to your next opportunity.

In Chapter 5, we discussed Effective Communication and Having High Integrity. Your words have power. Integrity in communication means standing by your word, being transparent, and ensuring that your message is understood. People respect those who are honest, articulate, and true to their values.

In Chapter 6, we talked about Networking Expansion and Building Good Relationships. Your network is your net worth. Opportunities don't come from isolation; they come from connections. The Dark Horse Mindset understands that relationships are built on trust, mutual respect, and genuine value.

In Chapter 7, we highlighted Building Trust and Integrity and Choosing the Right Partner. Trust is earned, not given, and the people you surround yourself with will shape your future. Choose wisely.

In Chapter 8, we emphasized the importance of Being an Expert on Something and Taking the Risk. The Dark Horse doesn't settle for mediocrity. If you want to stand out, you have to take risks, invest in your skills, and put in the hours to become an expert.

In Chapter 9, we covered Giving Value and Self-Love. You can't pour from an empty cup. The more you invest in yourself, your growth, well-being, and knowledge, the more you have to offer others.

In Chapter 10, we delved into Negotiation and Persuasion and Going the Extra Mile. The world belongs to those who are willing to do what others won't. The Dark Horse Mindset means pushing harder, staying prepared, and never settling for less than what you're worth.

And finally, in Chapter 11, we discussed Accept and Move Forward. We broke down how to stop dwelling on the past, let go of what you can't control, and focus on what actually moves you forward. Setbacks happen to everyone, but the people who succeed are the ones who learn from them and keep going. It's all about shifting your mindset, bouncing back stronger, and making sure every step you take is toward something better.

Throughout this book, we've talked about self-awareness, resilience, and mastering the skills needed to navigate life's toughest battles.

But at the core of it all, the most important lesson is this: You are in control of your own story.

No one is coming to save you. No one is going to hand you the life you dream of. That responsibility belongs to you; it's in your hands and yours alone.

This book was never about me. It was about you. Your potential. Your untapped greatness. Your ability to transform setbacks into stepping stones and carve out a path uniquely your own.

So, as you close this book, I ask you.

What will you do next?

Will you go back to your old ways, letting fear and doubt dictate your decisions?

Or will you step up and take control of your future?

Because the truth is, everything you need is already inside you.

The only question left is, will you have the courage to use it?

SNAPSHOTS OF THE JOURNEY

For every lesson in these pages, there was a real moment that shaped it...

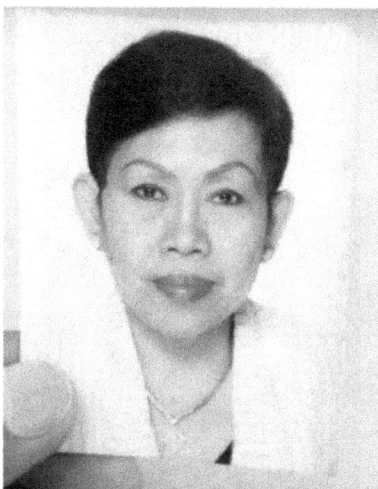

Picture of mom before she passed away, battling cancer for 11 years.

The dad I never saw.

The version of me (1983) and my mom.

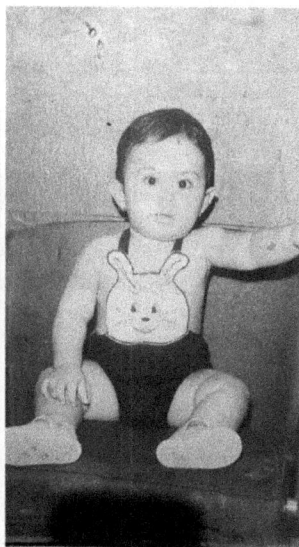

It's me again, 1984

CHAPTER ONE

ME IN 2024

WAKEBOARD DAYS

The face behind the mindset.

This was the time that I was featured in an international wakeboarding magazine

Gerald
esmailzadeh
height 5'8.5" vital stats: 38"-29"-36" hair

Gerald
esmailzadeh

MODELING DAYS

CHAPTER TWO

171

FAMILY PHOTO

Christmas Snapshot...

My whole heart
in one frame.

FROM FIT...

TO UNFIT.
Pandemic Time

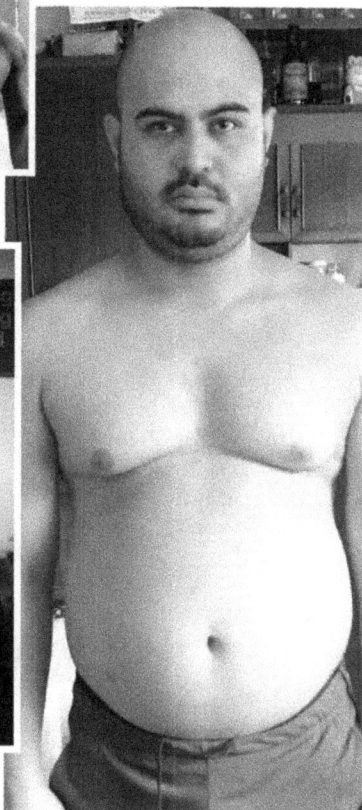

Hermit Mode
Pandemic Time

Every body tells a story. This one lived through a pandemic and made it out stronger.

This is **THE SHOES** in Chapter 3...

PANDEMIC PROJECT

Not just directing camera, but also directing energy.

CHAPTER THREE

BTS PAPER ST. SHOOT

Doing what I love to do...

TEAM
AWARDS

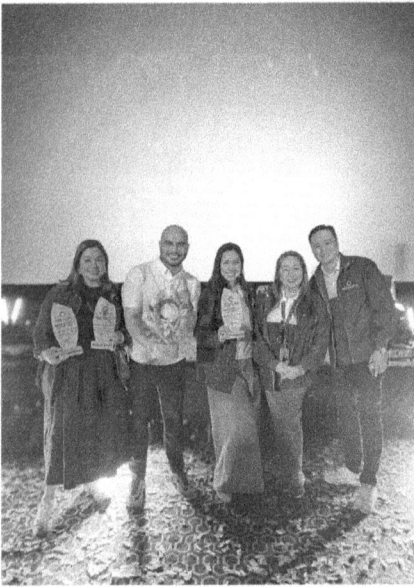

Everyone on my team ranked #1—Hard work, late nights, and a little bit of magic. ✦

CHAPTER FOUR AND FIVE

THE STUDIO AND OFFICE OF PAPER ST.

From blank walls to bold visions. This is where it all happens.

177

BEING A SALESMAN IN THE
CAR INDUSTRY

This guy was my first client...

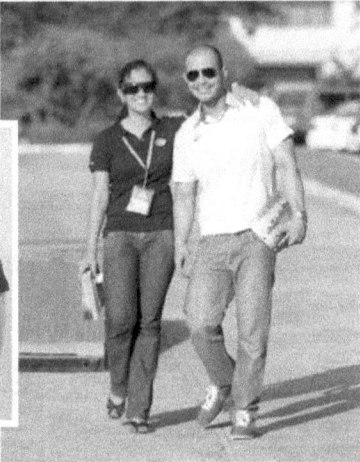

NOV. 1 STORY
— From Client to Friends

OVERALL TOP #1 SALES DIRECTOR

CHAPTER NINE

Got promoted (2025) and still pushing for the best version of me.

PODTRUCK
GRAND LAUNCH

From a wild idea to wheels on the ground—this was just the beginning.

CHAPTER NINE

IN MY ELEMENT

Every crowd, every mic, every moment—I show up all in.

An episode with celebrities...

One of Southeast Asia's Leading Inspirational Speakers

THE MEGA MALL STORY

She didn't know she was changing my life that night —neither did I.

A quiet reminder that behind every breakthrough start with the ones who believed in you first.

LIFE OVER WHISKEY

First time to meet my Co-Host.
Pandemic Project

←

Life Over Whiskey Grand Launch

at McKinley Whisky Park, BGC (Asia's first
and largest outdoor whisky venue, nestled
just beside BGC in Taguig, Metro Manila.)

The day we interviewed a 109 Year-Old Legend

ME AND MY
FIRST BORN

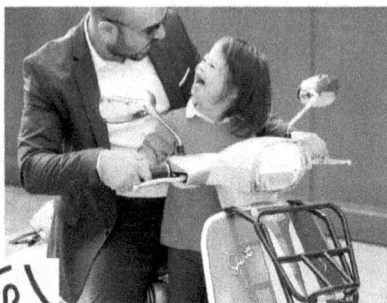

TYLER'S BORN DAY

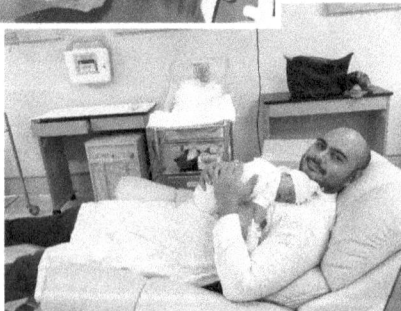

He didn't come into the world the way I expected—but he came exactly the way I needed.

184

SM Mall of Asia

Just like daddy, my son representing Philippines for World Down Syndrome Day

ME AND CHAY

My life partner, my anchor.

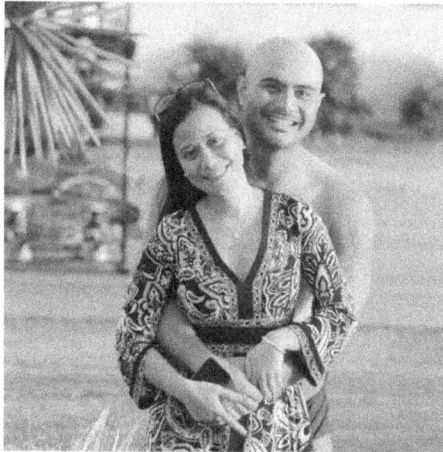

"LAGMAN FAMILY"

Thank you for opening your hearts and home to me.
You've given me more than friendship—you've given me
family.

The girl from Chapter 5—big heart, big
house, and yes... the car too.

JUST ME

Half shadow.
half light.
100% real.

AYO CREATIVES

Creative chaos, powered
by heart and hustle.

COMPETING IN
KETTLE BELL
SPORTS

Thank you so much for choosing this book and allowing it to be a part of your journey.

It means so much to me that you've invested your time, energy, and heart into these pages. My hope is that this book has encouraged you, inspired you, or helped you in some small (or big) way.

Every reader is special to me, and I am truly grateful for your support. Your willingness to grow, reflect, and show up for yourself is something to be proud of.

If you enjoyed this book, I would greatly appreciate it if you could simply leave a review on Amazon by scanning the QR code.

Your feedback helps others discover this book and supports my work in creating more resources like this.

Thank you again for being here. I am honored to be a small part of your story.

With gratitude,

GERALD ESMAILZADEH

Scan the QR code to leave a review:

ACKNOWLEDGMENT

This book is dedicated to my mom, my wife, and my two boys. They are my biggest inspirations.

Mom, for teaching me resilience and hard work. My wife, for standing by me through every crazy idea and late-night grind. And my boys, for reminding me every day why I push forward. Everything I do is for you.

I also want to thank the people who have supported me along the way, the Lagman family and my Aunt Cory, or "Tita Cory," who always had my back. She may no longer be here, but her love and guidance stay with me.

To my family and friends, the ones who've shaped me, challenged me, and stood by me. This book is for you.

To everyone who's helped me get to where I am, you know who you are. I don't need to name names but just know I appreciate you.

And to you, dear reader, wherever you are in your journey, I hope this book gives you something valuable. Maybe a new perspective, maybe a push to keep going. If there's one thing I've learned, it's this: your story is still being written, and you have the power to shape it.

Keep pushing, keep growing, and most of all, keep believing in yourself.

ABOUT THE AUTHOR

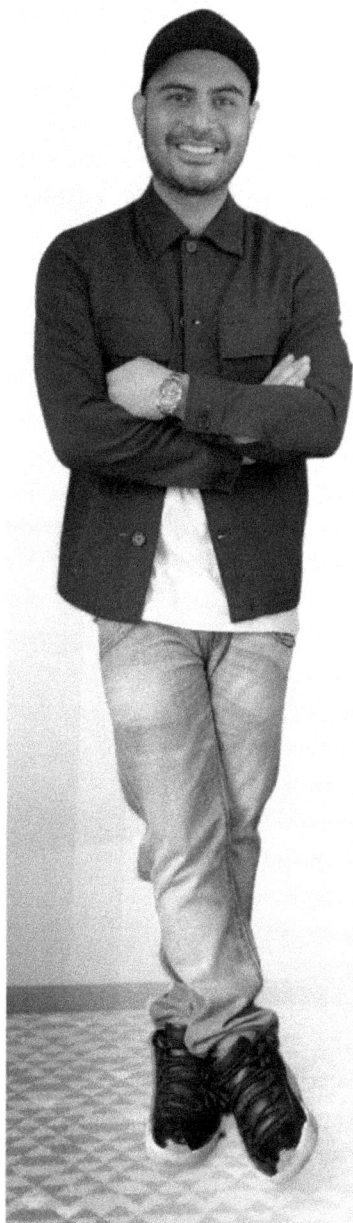

Gerald Esmailzadeh's journey has been anything but conventional. From his early days as a model to transitioning into real estate and creatives, he has worn many hats throughout his career, but at the core of it all, he found his true calling—storytelling.

This led him to launch his own company, Paper St Production, a premiere production company specializing in high-quality videos. His relentless pursuit of creative mastery led him to direct commercials for multinational companies.

Outside of video production, Gerald has built a name in other industries. He's the host of "Life Over Whiskey," a podcast where he and his co-host dive into real, unfiltered conversations about life that give value to listeners. He is also one of the founders of AYO Creatives, an advertising agency that helps brands craft impactful stories through innovative marketing and content creation. On top of that, he co-founded PodTruck, the Philippines' first and only roving podcast studio—giving brands, creators, and storytellers a space to share and amplify their voices wherever they may be.

In the corporate world, Gerald has over 20 years of extensive experience in the real estate industry. His expertise and leadership have earned him the title of #1 Senior Sales Director for three consecutive years.
He is an advocate for a healthy plant-based lifestyle and keeps fitness a priority. He's also passionate about Down syndrome awareness, dedicating his time and resources to supporting the community.

Gerald believes in the power of discipline—not just in his career but in all aspects of life. His life is a testament to taking risks, pushing boundaries, and creating value wherever he goes.

ntent.com/pod-product-compliance
/ce LLC
g PA
21040426
300012B/2760